GW01005447

The Dover Opera Libretto Series

VERDI'S
RIGOLETTO

GIUSEPPE VERDI

Introduced and Translated by
ELLEN H. BLEILER

DOVER PUBLICATIONS, INC.
NEW YORK

Published in Canada by General Publishing Company, Ltd., 30 Lesmill Road, Don Mills, Toronto, Ontario.
Published in the United Kingdom by Constable and Company, Ltd.

This Dover edition, first published in 1983, contains the standard Italian libretto of *Rigoletto*, accompanied by a complete new English translation prepared specially for Dover Publications by Ellen H. Bleiler, together with an introduction and plot summary by Ms. Bleiler.

Manufactured in the United States of America
Dover Publications, Inc., 180 Varick Street, New York, N.Y. 10014

Library of Congress Cataloging in Publication Data

Verdi, Giuseppe, 1813–1901.
[Rigoletto. Libretto. English & Italian]
Verdi's Rigoletto.

(The Dover opera libretto series)
English and Italian.
Based on: Le roi s'amuse / Victor Hugo.
Libretto by Francesco Maria Piave.
1. Operas—Librettos. I. Bleiler, Ellen H. II. Piave, Francesco Maria, 1810–1876. III. Hugo, Victor, 1802–1885. Roi s'amuse. IV. Title. V. Title: Rigoletto. VI. Series.
ML50.V484R52 1983 782.1'2 82-18194
ISBN 0-486-24497-0

CONTENTS

INTRODUCTION

Near the beginning of *Rigoletto*, some of the courtiers say of their debauched master: "And thus the Duke amuses himself." Perhaps these words were Verdi's way of acknowledging his debt to Victor Hugo. In 1851, Verdi turned Hugo's play *Le Roi s'amuse* (The King Amuses Himself) into an opera. At the behest of nervous Austrian censors, he also turned "Le Roi" of the title, Francis I of France, into the Duke of Mantua.

Hugo's play was first staged in Paris in 1832. It owed what little fame it had to being closed on the second night by the censors, who found it lewd, indecent and disrespectful to royalty. Almost twenty years later, the opera based on Hugo's play was still considered raunchy. In addition, church officials found Verdi's original title for it, "La Maledizione" (The Curse), blasphemous. But the Austrian censors who had to approve whatever was performed at Venice's Fenice Theater were chiefly concerned with the opera's portrait of an historical French king (1494–1547) as an irresponsible profligate. It was, after all, less than three years since a contemporary French king had been forced by revolutionaries to flee his country, and just over fifty years since an earlier French king was beheaded by his countrymen. Obviously, royalty could be toppled all too easily without the aid of a popular living composer.

Verdi was not especially happy about making the changes that the censors demanded. Besides turning Francis into the nameless Duke, he also changed Francis's historical jester Triboulet (Italian: Triboletto) into Rigoletto, and the jester's fictitious daughter Blanche/Bianca into Gilda. After the censors and Verdi managed to resolve still further squabbles, the opera was finally produced at the Fenice on March 11, 1851. It was immediately a huge success, receiving twenty-one performances that season and even more the next. It was soon sung throughout Italy and in most other countries of Europe except France, where the exiled Victor Hugo, annoyed that Verdi had succeeded where he himself had failed, fought to keep it off the boards. Hugo lost his battle, and in 1857 *Rigoletto* was performed in the Italian Theater of Paris. Years later, some friends finally persuaded Hugo to attend, and the playwright's bitterness vanished in his warm admiration for Verdi's music. In 1855, *Rigoletto* was performed at the New York Academy of Music, and finally in 1883, at the Metropolitan Opera, where it remains a favorite.

Rigoletto was the sixteenth of Verdi's twenty-six operas, and his sixth collaboration with the librettist Piave. As with most of the dramas he set to music, Verdi did not worry about the lunatic improbability of the plot, but was intrigued by the complex and contradictory qualities of a particular character. For almost the first time, Verdi tried to write music that would define personality. That he succeeded in doing this is apparent in the Act Four quartet, where each participant expresses himself in a distinctly individual melodic line. On hearing the quartet, Victor Hugo is supposed to have said that if he could only have let four characters speak at the same time on stage, his play would have been as successful as the opera.

Despite the more advanced technique of *Rigoletto* in comparison with its predecessors, Verdi's music is still criticized for its horsiness in some passages and its wailing cellos in others. Certainly, just as in much of Verdi's earlier work, the music's drive and vigor outweigh its subtleties. Still, *Rigoletto* does have subtleties. One example is the sudden modulation that changes the closing cadences of "Questo o quella" into a decadently sweet minuet, anticipating the Duke's own repeated shifts from general bravado to specific desire. Other musical nuances become apparent whenever a conductor is strong enough to integrate the opera's leading parts rather than allowing each singer to perform his arias as though he were giving a solo recital.

The opera's plot is undoubtedly highly melodramatic and its characterizations also receive their share of sneers. Rigoletto's switches from vicious pander to doting parent are hard to swallow even for those who acknowledge the pathos in Act Four. And Gilda is almost invariably dismissed as a ninny—but allowances should be made even for her. For one thing, modern opera-goers probably imagine Gilda older than Victor Hugo intended, for twentieth-century audiences dislike associating nubility with a girl in her early teens and forget that Juliet herself was only fourteen when she met Romeo. Gilda becomes less improbable when one remembers that she doubtless spent all her life in a convent school where the idea of sacrificing oneself for someone else would have been regarded with favor. Furthermore, since Rigoletto did not even choose to tell Gilda his name, it is highly unlikely that he would have discussed the facts of life with her.

PLOT SUMMARY

Rigoletto is an opera in four acts, although the first act is so short that it is usually treated as a scene and followed by the second act without intermission.

ACT ONE

During a party in his palace, the Duke of Mantua tells his courtiers that he would like to conclude his escapade with a beautiful unknown girl whom he has been seeing in church. At the same time, the Duke admires Countess Ceprano. Rigoletto maliciously suggests abducting the Countess and recommends ways to get rid of the angry and jealous Count Ceprano. Marullo excitedly tells the other courtiers that Rigoletto actually has what Marullo believes to be a mistress. Ceprano, enraged at Rigoletto's taunts, is just drawing his sword when Monterone bursts in and berates the Duke for seducing his daughter. Rigoletto mocks Monterone who curses Duke, jester and courtiers. Ceprano urges all who bear Rigoletto a grudge to seek revenge that evening, while Rigoletto flinches in horror at Monterone's curse.

ACT TWO

On his way home, Rigoletto broods about Monterone's curse. As he reaches his house, the jester is accosted by the assassin Sparafucile, who offers his professional services. Rigoletto refuses—for the moment. Entering his garden, the jester is met by his affectionate daughter Gilda and her maid. Both women assure Rigoletto that his daughter has remained completely secluded; they do not mention the young man whom Gilda has been seeing at church. The Duke slips into the garden and hides until Rigoletto leaves. Then the Duke and Gilda declare love for each other, she believing him to be a poor student. When courtiers gather in the street, the Duke, fearing discovery, leaves. Rigoletto returns, and the courtiers pretend to seek his help in abducting Countess Ceprano. They blindfold him, and he holds their ladder. The courtiers seize Gilda, and the horrified Rigoletto realizes that he has been duped into helping to abduct his own daughter.

ACT THREE

In the palace, the Duke wonders what has become of Gilda. The courtiers enter and tell how they tricked Rigoletto into helping kidnap the girl whom they believe to be his mistress. The Duke, realizing that his lost love and Rigoletto's supposed mistress are one and the same, rushes to the girl. Rigoletto enters, feigning nonchalance but looking everywhere for his daughter. When the courtiers suggest that he seek his mistress elsewhere, Rigoletto turns on them in a rage and demands his daughter. Gilda runs to her father from a room on the side. Rigoletto peremptorily sends the courtiers away, and Gilda tells her father how the Duke wooed her and the courtiers abducted her and brought her to the palace, where the Duke seduced her. Rigoletto vows to be avenged.

ACT FOUR

At Mantua's outskirts, Rigoletto and Gilda wait outside the ramshackle inn belonging to Sparafucile and his sister Maddalena. The Duke arrives; Sparafucile slips outside to ask Rigoletto whether this is indeed the man whom the jester wants killed. The Duke flirts with Maddalena, and Gilda realizes how meaningless were his declarations of love to herself. But the heartbroken girl loves him still. Rigoletto sends Gilda home to dress herself in male attire and go from Mantua. A storm gathers, and Rigoletto leaves, saying he will return at midnight. The Duke goes to bed.

Maddalena begs Sparafucile not to kill the young man. Sparafucile insists that he has been paid to murder the Duke and intends to keep his bargain. Gilda returns just in time to hear brother and sister agree that if anyone comes to the inn before midnight, Sparafucile will take his life in place of the Duke's. Impulsively, Gilda knocks at the inn door just as the storm reaches its height.

Just before midnight, Rigoletto returns to receive a body in a sack from Sparafucile. As he prepares to throw the sack into the river, the jester hears the Duke's voice. Mystified, Rigoletto opens the sack and to his horror finds his dying daughter inside it. Gilda begs her father's forgiveness and dies. The despairing jester again recalls Monterone's curse and collapses on his child's body.

RIGOLETTO

Opera in Four Acts

Music by Giuseppe Verdi

Libretto by Francesco Maria Piave

CHARACTERS

THE DUKE OF MANTUA	Tenor
BORSA, a courtier	Tenor
THE COUNTESS OF CEPRANO	Mezzo-soprano
RIGOLETTO, the Duke's hunchbacked jester	Baritone
COUNT CEPRANO	Bass
MARULLO, a courtier	Baritone
COUNT MONTERONE	Baritone
SPARAFUCILE, a professional assassin	Bass
GILDA, daughter of Rigoletto	Soprano
GIOVANNA, maid to Gilda	Mezzo-soprano
A PAGE AT THE COURT	Soprano
A HERALD	Baritone
MADDALENA, sister of Sparafucile	Contralto

Courtiers, ladies, servants, soldiers.

Mantua, in the sixteenth century.

ACT ONE

ACT ONE

A brightly lighted ballroom in the DUKE's *palace. Some lords and ladies dance; other lords and ladies, ushers and pages cross back and forth. The* DUKE *and* BORSA *appear, talking to each other.*

DUKE: Della mia bella incognita borghese toccare il fin dell'avventura io voglio.	DUKE: I want to wind up the affair with my beautiful unknown townswoman.
BORSA: Di quella giovin che vedete al tempio?	BORSA: With the young person whom you see at church?
DUKE: Da tre mesi ogni festa.	DUKE: Every holy day for three months.
BORSA: La sua dimora?	BORSA: Her dwelling place?
DUKE: In un remoto calle; misterioso un uom v'entra ogni notte.	DUKE: In a distant street; a mysterious man goes there every night.
BORSA: E sa colei chi sia l'amante suo?	BORSA: And does she know who her suitor is?
DUKE: Lo ignora.	DUKE: She doesn't know.

Lords and ladies cross the stage.

BORSA: Quante beltà! Mirate.	BORSA: How many beauties! Look.
DUKE: Le vince tutte di Cepran la sposa.	DUKE: Ceprano's wife outdoes them all.
BORSA *(aside)*: Non v'oda il Conte, o Duca.	BORSA *(aside)*: Don't let the Count hear you, Duke.

DUKE: A me che importa?

BORSA: Dirlo ad altra ei potria.

DUKE: Nè sventura per me certo saria. Questa o quella per me pari sono a quant'altre d'intorno, d'intorno mi vedo; del mio core l'impero non cedo meglio ad una, che ad altra beltà. La costoro avvenenza è qual dono di che il fato ne infiora la vita; s'oggi questa mi torna gradita, forse un'altra, forse un'altra doman lo sarà, un'altra, forse un'altra doman lo sarà. La costanza, tiranna del core, detestiamo qual morbo, qual morbo crudele; sol chi vuole si serbi fedele. Non v'ha amor, se non v'è libertà. De' mariti il geloso furore, degli amanti le smanie derido; anco d'Argo i cent'occhi disfido se mi punge, se mi punge una qualche beltà, se mi punge una qualche beltà.

DUKE: What do I care?

BORSA: He might tell another woman.

DUKE: Nor would that be such a misfortune for me. This one or that one are the same to me as all the other women I see about me, about me; I don't let one beauty rule my heart any more than another. Their comeliness is like a gift with which fate ornaments our life. If this one finds favor with me today, perhaps tomorrow it will be another, perhaps another, perhaps tomorrow it will be another, perhaps another. Constancy, tyrant of the heart, we hate you like the plague, like the cruel plague, let them remain faithful who wish to; there's no love where there's no freedom. I scorn the jealous rage of husbands and the frenzy of lovers. I'd brave even the hundred eyes of Argus if some beauty enticed me, enticed me, some beauty enticed me.

The music changes to a minuet. The DUKE *brings forward the* COUNTESS CEPRANO *and addresses her with great gallantry.*

DUKE: Partite? Crudele!

COUNTESS CEPRANO: Seguire lo sposo m'è forza a Ceprano.

DUKE: You're leaving? Cruel one!

COUNTESS CEPRANO: I must follow my husband to Ceprano.

DUKE: Ma dee luminoso in corte tal astro qual sole brillare, per voi qui ciascuno dovrà palpitare. Per voi già possente la fiamma d'amore inebria *(He kisses her hand enthusiastically)*, conquide, distrugge il mio core.

DUKE: But such a luminary ought to shine at court like the sun; everyone's heart must throb for you. Already the powerful flame of my love for you intoxicates *(He kisses her hand enthusiastically)*, overpowers, destroys my heart.

COUNTESS CEPRANO: Calmatevi.

COUNTESS CEPRANO: Calm yourself.

DUKE: La fiamma d'amore inebria, conquide, distrugge il mio core!

DUKE: The flame of love intoxicates, overpowers, destroys my heart.

COUNTESS CEPRANO: Calmatevi, calmatevi.
DUKE: Per voi già possente—

COUNTESS CEPRANO: Calm yourself, calm yourself.
DUKE: Already the powerful flame of my love for you—

DUKE: —la fiamma d'amore inebria, conquide, distrugge il mio core!

DUKE: —intoxicates, overpowers, destroys my heart!

The DUKE *gives his arm to the* COUNTESS, *and they go out together.*

RIGOLETTO *(to* COUNT CEPRANO*)*: In testa che avete, signor di Ceprano?

RIGOLETTO *(to* COUNT CEPRANO*)*: What's that on your mind, lord of Ceprano?

With an impatient gesture, CEPRANO *follows the* DUKE. RIGOLETTO *turns to the courtiers.*

RIGOLETTO: Ei sbuffa! Vedete?

RIGOLETTO: He's fuming! You see?

BORSA & CHORUS: Che festa!

BORSA & CHORUS: What a to-do!

RIGOLETTO: Oh sì!

RIGOLETTO: Oh, yes!

BORSA & CHORUS: Il Duca qui pur si diverte!

BORSA: Thus the Duke amuses himself!

RIGOLETTO: Così non è sempre? Che nuove scoperte! Il giuoco ed il vino, le feste, la danza, battaglie, conviti, ben tutto gli sta. Or della Contessa l'assedio egli avanza, e intanto il marito fremendo ne va.	RIGOLETTO: Isn't it always so? What else is new! The gaming and the wine, the merry-making, the dancing, the fighting, feasting, he's always at them. Now he's laying siege to the Countess, and meanwhile her husband is boiling about it.

A Perigordino is danced on stage.*

MARULLO *(entering excitedly)*: Gran nuova! gran nuova!	MARULLO *(entering excitedly)*: Great news! great news!
BORSA & CHORUS: Che avvenne? parlate!	BORSA & CHORUS: What's happening? Speak!
MARULLO: Stupir ne dovrete—	MARULLO: You'll have to be astounded—
BORSA & CHORUS: Narrate, narrate!	BORSA & CHORUS: Tell, tell!
MARULLO *(laughing)*: Ah! ah! Rigoletto—	MARULLO *(laughing)*: Ha! ha! Rigoletto—
BORSA & CHORUS: Ebben?	BORSA & CHORUS: Well?
MARULLO: Caso enorme!	MARULLO: A tremendous thing!
BORSA & CHORUS: Perduto ha la gobba? Non è più difforme?	BORSA & CHORUS: Has he lost his hump? Is he no longer deformed?
MARULLO: Più strana è la cosa! Il pazzo possiede—	MARULLO: The thing is even stranger! The madman has—
BORSA & CHORUS: Infine?	BORSA & CHORUS: Well?
MARULLO: Un'amante!	MARULLO: A lover!
BORSA & CHORUS: Un'amante! Chi il crede?	BORSA & CHORUS: A lover! Who would have believed it!
MARULLO: Il gobbo in Cupido or s'è trasformato.	MARULLO: Now the hunchback has changed himself into Cupid.

* An old country dance in 6/8 time.

BORSA & CHORUS: Quel mostro? Cupido!	BORSA & CHORUS: That monster? Cupid!
MARULLO, BORSA & CHORUS: Cupido beato!	MARULLO, BORSA & CHORUS: Blessed Cupid!

The DUKE *reenters with* RIGOLETTO.

DUKE *(to* RIGOLETTO*)*: Ah più di Ceprano importuno non v'è! La cara sua sposa è un angiol per me!	DUKE *(to* RIGOLETTO*)*: No, there's no one more tiresome than Ceprano! To me, his precious wife's an angel!
RIGOLETTO: Rapitela.	RIGOLETTO: Run away with her.
DUKE: È detto; ma il farlo?	DUKE: Easy to say; but how to do it?
RIGOLETTO: Stasera.	RIGOLETTO: Tonight.
DUKE: Non pensi tu al Conte?	DUKE: Haven't you thought of the Count?
RIGOLETTO: Non c'è la prigione?	RIGOLETTO: Isn't there a prison?
DUKE: Ah no.	DUKE: Ah, no.
RIGOLETTO: Ebben—s'esilia.	RIGOLETTO: Well, then—exile him.
DUKE: Nemmeno, buffone.	DUKE: Not that either, clown.
RIGOLETTO: Allora—allora la testa—	RIGOLETTO: Then—then his head—

He makes a gesture as if decapitating someone.

CEPRANO *(aside)*: (Oh, l'anima nera!)	CEPRANO *(aside)*: (Oh, the blackguard!)
DUKE *(to* CEPRANO*)*: Che di', questa testa?	DUKE *(to* CEPRANO*)*: What do you say, this head?
RIGOLETTO: È ben naturale! Che far di tal testa? A cosa ella vale?	RIGOLETTO: It's a matter of course! What does such a head matter? What's it worth?

CEPRANO *(angrily reaching for his sword)*: Marrano!

DUKE *(to* CEPRANO*)*: Fermate!

RIGOLETTO: Da rider mi fa.

MARULLO & CHORUS: In furia è montato!

DUKE *(to* RIGOLETTO*)*: Buffone, vien qua.

BORSA: In furia è montato!

MARULLO: In furia è montato!

CHORUS: In furia è montato!

DUKE *(to* RIGOLETTO*)*: Ah! sempre tu spingi—

DUKE: —lo scherzo all'estremo.

CEPRANO *(to courtiers)*: Vendetta del pazzo!—

CEPRANO: —Contr'esso un rancore di noi chi non ha?

RIGOLETTO: Che coglier mi puote? Di loro non temo.

DUKE: Quell'ira che sfidi colpir ti potrà.

CEPRANO: Vendetta!

BORSA, MARULLO, CHORUS: Ma come?

CEPRANO: In armi chi ha core doman sia da me, a notte.

BORSA, MARULLO, CHORUS: Sì, sarà!

RIGOLETTO: Del Duca il protetto nessun toccherà.

CEPRANO *(angrily reaching for his sword)*: Peasant!

DUKE *(to* CEPRANO*)*: Stay!

RIGOLETTO: He makes me laugh.

MARULLO & CHORUS: He's getting furious!

DUKE *(to* RIGOLETTO*)*: Clown, come here.

BORSA: He's getting furious!

MARULLO: He's getting furious!

CHORUS: He's getting furious!

DUKE *(to* RIGOLETTO*)*: Ah! you're always carrying—

DUKE: —the joke too far.

CEPRANO *(to courtiers)*: Vengeance on the madman!—

CEPRANO: —Which of us doesn't bear him a grudge?

RIGOLETTO: What can happen to me? I'm not afraid of them.

DUKE: That rage which you defy may strike you down.

CEPRANO: Vengeance!

BORSA, MARULLO, CHORUS: But how?

CEPRANO: Tomorrow evening, let whoever has the courage come to my home armed.

BORSA, MARULLO, CHORUS: Yes, it will be so!

RIGOLETTO: Nobody will touch one who's under the Duke's protection.

DUKE: Ah, sempre tu spingi lo scherzo all'estremo, ah, sempre tu spingi lo scherzo all'estremo, quell'ira che sfidi, quell'ira che sfidi colpirti potrà. Ah, sempre tu spingi lo scherzo all'estremo, ah, sempre tu spingi lo scherzo all'estremo, quell'ira che sfidi, quell'ira che sfidi colpirti potrà!

DUKE: Ah, you're always carrying the joke too far, ah, you're always carrying the joke too far, that rage which you defy, that rage which you defy may strike you down. Ah, you're always carrying the joke too far, ah, you're always carrying the joke too far, that rage which you defy, that rage which you defy may strike you down!

RIGOLETTO: Che coglier mi puote? Di loro non temo, del Duca il protetto nessun toccherà, no, no, nessun, nessuno, nessun, nessuno, nessun, nessuno del Duca il protetto, nessuno toccherà. Che coglier mi puote? Di loro non temo, del Duca il protetto nessun toccherà, no, no, nessun, nessuno, nessun, nessuno, nessun, nessuno del Duca il protetto, nessuno toccherà.

RIGOLETTO: What can happen to me? I'm not afraid of them, nobody will touch one who's under the Duke's protection, no, no, nobody, nobody, nobody, nobody, nobody, nobody, nobody will touch one who's under the Duke's protection. What can happen to me? I'm not afraid of them, nobody will touch one who's under the Duke's protection, no, no, nobody, nobody, nobody, nobody, nobody, nobody, nobody will touch one who's under the Duke's protection.

BORSA, MARULLO, CEPRANO, CHORUS: Vendetta del pazzo! Contr'esso un rancore pei tristi suoi modi di noi chi non ha? Vendetta! vendetta! vendetta!—

BORSA, MARULLO, CEPRANO, CHORUS: Vengeance on the madman! Which of us doesn't bear him a grudge for his wicked ways? Vengeance! vengeance! vengeance!—

CEPRANO: —stanotte chi ha core sia in armi da me. Vendetta del pazzo! Contr'esso un rancore pei tristi suoi modi di noi chi non ha? Vendetta! vendetta! vendetta! stanotte chi ha core sia in armi da me.

CEPRANO: —Let whoever has the courage come armed to my home tonight. Vengeance on the madman! Which of us doesn't bear him a grudge for his wicked ways? Vengeance! vengeance! vengeance! Let whoever has the courage come armed to my home tonight.

BORSA, MARULLO, CHORUS: —sì, è detto—sarà. Vendetta del pazzo! Contr'esso un rancore pei tristi suoi modi di noi chi non ha? Vendetta! vendetta! vendetta! sì, è detto, sarà.

BORSA, MARULLO, CHORUS: —yes, no sooner said than done. Vengeance on the madman! Which of us doesn't bear him a grudge for his wicked ways? Vengeance! vengeance! vengeance! yes, no sooner said than done.

BORSA, TENORS: Sì, vendetta!

BORSA, TENORS: Yes, vengeance!

MARULLO, TENORS: Sì, vendetta!

MARULLO, TENORS: Yes, vengeance!

CEPRANO, BASSES: Sì, vendetta!

CEPRANO, BASSES: Yes, vengeance!

DUKE & RIGOLETTO: Tutto è gioia!

DUKE & RIGOLETTO: Everything is joyful!

BORSA, TENORS: Sì, vendetta!

BORSA, TENORS: Yes, vengeance!

MARULLO, TENORS: Sì, vendetta!

MARULLO, TENORS: Yes, vengeance!

CEPRANO, BASSES: Sì, vendetta!

CEPRANO, BASSES: Yes, vengeance!

DUKE & RIGOLETTO: Tutto è festa—

DUKE & RIGOLETTO: Everything is festive—

ALL: —tutto è gioia, tutto è festa; tutto invitaci a godere! Oh guardate, non par questa or la reggia del piacere! Oh

ALL: —everything is joyful, everything is festive; everything bids us rejoice! Oh look, doesn't this seem indeed the

guardate, non par questa, oh guardate, non par questa or la reggia del piacer! Oh guardate, non par questa or la reggia del piacer!

palace of pleasure! Oh look, doesn't this seem, oh look, doesn't this seem indeed the palace of pleasure! Oh look, doesn't this seem indeed the palace of pleasure!

MONTERONE'S *voice is heard offstage; he enters.*

MONTERONE: Ch'io gli parli.

MONTERONE: Let me speak to him.

DUKE: No!

DUKE: No!

MONTERONE: Il voglio.

MONTERONE: I will.

RIGOLETTO, BORSA, MARULLO, CEPRANO, CHORUS: Monterone!

RIGOLETTO, BORSA, MARULLO, CEPRANO, CHORUS: Monterone!

MONTERONE: Sì, Monteron—la voce mia qual tuono vi scuoterà dovunque.

MONTERONE: Yes, Monterone—like thunder my voice will make you tremble wherever you may be.

RIGOLETTO *(mimicking* MONTERONE*)*: Ch'io gli parli. Voi congiuraste, voi congiuraste contro noi, signore; e noi, e noi clementi in vero, perdonammo ... Qual vi piglia or delirio, a tutte l'ore di vostra figlia a reclamar l'onore?

RIGOLETTO *(mimicking* MONTERONE*)*: Let me speak to him. You conspired, you conspired against us, sir; and we, and we, truly merciful, forgave ... What madness now drives you to complain constantly about your daughter's honor?

MONTERONE *(looking at* RIGOLETTO *with contempt)*: Novello insulto! *(To the* DUKE:*)* Ah sì, a turbare, ah sì, a turbare sarò vostr'orgie ... verrò a gridare fino a che vegga restarsi inulto di mia famiglia l'atroce insulto; e se al carnefice pur mi darete, spettro terribile mi rivedrete,

MONTERONE *(looking at* RIGOLETTO *with contempt)*: A fresh insult! *(To the* DUKE:*)* Ah yes, I'm going to disturb, ah yes, to disturb your debaucheries ... I will shout out as long as the vile insult to my family remains unpunished; and if you hand me to the executioner, you'll

portante in mano il teschio mio, vendetta a chiedere, vendetta a chiedere al mondo, al mondo, a Dio.

DUKE: Non più, arrestatelo!

RIGOLETTO: È matto!

BORSA, MARULLO, CEPRANO: Quai detti!

MONTERONE (*to the* DUKE & RIGOLETTO): Ah, siate entrambi voi maledetti!

BORSA, MARULLO, CEPRANO, CHORUS: Ah!

MONTERONE: Slanciare il cane a leon morente è vile, o Duca ... (*Turning to* RIGOLETTO:) e tu, serpente, tu che d'un padre ridi al dolore, sii maledetto!

RIGOLETTO (*wincing in horror*): (Che sento! orrore!)

DUKE, BORSA, MARULLO, CEPRANO, CHORUS: Oh, tu che la festa audace hai turbato, da un genio d'inferno qui fosti guidato;—

RIGOLETTO: (Orrore!)

DUKE, BORSA, MARULLO, CEPRANO, CHORUS: —è vano ogni detto, di qua t'allontana ... va, trema, o vegliardo, dell'ira sovrana ... è vano ogni detto, di qua t'allontana ... va, trema, o vegliardo, dell'ira sovrana, tu l'hai provocata, più speme non v'è, un'ora fatale fu questa per

see my dreadful spectre bearing my skull in its hand, demanding vengeance, demanding vengeance of the world, of the world, of God.

DUKE: No more, seize him!

RIGOLETTO: He's mad!

BORSA, MARULLO, CEPRANO: Such words!

MONTERONE (*to the* DUKE & RIGOLETTO): Ah, a curse on you both!

BORSA, MARULLO, CEPRANO, CHORUS: Ah!

MONTERONE: To set your cur on a dying lion is vile, o Duke ... (*Turning to* RIGOLETTO:) and you, serpent, you that mock a father's sorrow, a curse on you!

RIGOLETTO (*wincing in horror*): (What do I hear! horror!)

DUKE, BORSA, MARULLO, CEPRANO, CHORUS: Oh, you who have dared to disturb our merrymaking, a devil from hell led you here;—

RIGOLETTO: (Horror!)

DUKE, BORSA, MARULLO, CEPRANO, CHORUS: —every word is in vain, begone from here ... Go, quake, old man, at the sovereign wrath ... every word is in vain, begone from here ... go, quake, old man, at the sovereign wrath you have provoked, there's no more hope,

te, un'ora fatale fu questa per te, fu questa per te,—

this was a fatal hour for you, this was, this was a fatal hour for you,—

MONTERONE: Sii maledetto! e tu serpente, tu che d'un padre ridi al dolore, sii maledetto! e tu serpente, tu che d'un padre ridi al dolore, sii maledetto! sii maledetto! sii maledetto! sii maledetto! sii maledetto!

MONTERONE: A curse on you! and you, serpent, you that mock a father's sorrow, a curse on you! and you, serpent, you that mock a father's sorrow, a curse on you! a curse on you! a curse on you! a curse on you! a curse on you!

RIGOLETTO: (Che orrore! che orrore! Ah! che orrore! che orror! ah! che orrore, che orror! orrore! orrore! orrore! che orror! che orror! che orror! che orror! che orror! che orror! che orror!)

RIGOLETTO: (What horror! what horror! Ah! what horror! what horror! Ah! what horror, what horror! horror! horror! horror! what horror! what horror! what horror! what horror! what horror! what horror! what horror!)

DUKE, BORSA, MARULLO, TENORS: —va, va, trema, va, va, trema, o vegliardo, più speme non v'è, va, va, trema, va, va, trema, o vegliardo, più speme non v'è, più speme non v'è, più speme non v'è, più speme non v'è, non v'è, non v'è, non v'è, non v'è, non v'è, non v'è, no, non v'è!

DUKE, BORSA, MARULLO, TENORS: —go, go, quake, go, go, quake, old man, there's no more hope, go, go, quake, go, go, quake, old man, there's no more hope, there's no more hope, there's no more hope, there's no more hope, there isn't, there isn't, there isn't, there isn't, there isn't, there isn't! no, there isn't!

CEPRANO & BASSES: —va, va, trema, o vegliardo, più speme non v'è, un'ora fatale fu questa per te, fu questa per te, va, va, trema, o vegliardo, più speme non v'è, un'ora fatale fu questa

CEPRANO & BASSES: —go, go, quake, old man, there's no more hope, this was, this was a fatal hour for you, go, go, quake, old man, there's no more hope, this was, this was a

per te, fu questa per te, più speme non v'è, più speme non v'è, più speme non v'è, non v'è, non v'è, non v'è, non v'è, non v'è, non v'è, no, non v'è!

fatal hour for you, there's no more hope, there's no more hope, there's no more hope, there isn't, there isn't, there isn't, there isn't, there isn't, there isn't, no, there isn't.

MONTERONE *is led out by two armed guards.*

ACT TWO

ACT TWO

The end of a deserted street. On one side is a house inside a walled courtyard with a garden seat. It is dusk. RIGOLETTO *appears, wrapped in his cloak. He is followed by* SPARAFUCILE, *who carries a long sword under his cape.*

RIGOLETTO: (Quel vecchio maledivami!)

SPARAFUCILE *(approaching)*: Signor—

RIGOLETTO: Va, non ho niente.

SPARAFUCILE: Nè il chiesi . . . A voi presente un uom di spada sta.

RIGOLETTO: Un ladro?

SPARAFUCILE: Un uom che libera per poco da un rivale, e voi ne avete—

RIGOLETTO: Quale?

SPARAFUCILE: La vostra donna è là.

RIGOLETTO: (Che sento!) E quanto spendere per un signor dovrei?

SPARAFUCILE: Prezzo maggior vorrei.

RIGOLETTO: (That old man cursed me!)

SPARAFUCILE *(approaching)*: Sir—

RIGOLETTO: Go away, I don't have anything.

SPARAFUCILE: Nor did I ask it . . . A man with a sword is now standing before you.

RIGOLETTO: A thief?

SPARAFUCILE: A man who, for a small consideration, will free you from a rival, and you have some—

RIGOLETTO: What?

SPARAFUCILE: Your lady is over there.

RIGOLETTO: (What do I hear!) And how much would it cost me for a gentleman?

SPARAFUCILE: I'd want a greater price.

RIGOLETTO: Com'usasi pagar?

RIGOLETTO: How are you usually paid?

SPARAFUCILE: Una metà s'anticipa, il resto si dà poi ...

SPARAFUCILE: One half beforehand, the rest afterwards ...

RIGOLETTO: (Demonio!) E come puoi tanto securo oprar?

RIGOLETTO: (Fiend!) And how can you work with such safety?

SPARAFUCILE: Soglio in cittade uccidere, oppure nel mio tetto. L'uomo di sera aspetto—una stoccata, e muor.

SPARAFUCILE: I usually kill in the city, or else under my own roof. I wait for the man in the evening—one thrust, and he dies.

RIGOLETTO: (Demonio!) E come in casa?

RIGOLETTO: (Fiend!) And how do you manage it in your house?

SPARAFUCILE: È facile ... m'aiuta mia sorella ... per le vie danza ... è bella ... Chi voglio attira ... e allor ...

SPARAFUCILE: It's easy ... my sister helps me ... she dances in the streets ... she's beautiful ... she lures whomever I want ... and then ...

RIGOLETTO: Comprendo.

RIGOLETTO: I understand.

SPARAFUCILE: Senza strepito ...

SPARAFUCILE: Without any racket ...

RIGOLETTO: Comprendo.

RIGOLETTO: I understand.

SPARAFUCILE *(drawing his sword)*: È questo il mio strumento. Vi serve?

SPARAFUCILE *(drawing his sword)*: This is my tool. Is it of use to you?

RIGOLETTO: No, al momento.

RIGOLETTO: Not at the moment.

SPARAFUCILE *(putting away his sword)*: Peggio per voi ...

SPARAFUCILE *(putting away his sword)*: The worse for you ...

RIGOLETTO: Chi sa?

RIGOLETTO: Who knows?

SPARAFUCILE: Sparafucil mi nomino ...

SPARAFUCILE: My name is Sparafucile ...

RIGOLETTO: Straniero?

RIGOLETTO: A foreigner?

SPARAFUCILE: Borgognone.

SPARAFUCILE: Burgundian.

RIGOLETTO: E dove, all'occasione?

SPARAFUCILE: Qui sempre a sera.

RIGOLETTO: Va.

SPARAFUCILE: Sparafucil, Sparafucil.

RIGOLETTO: Va, va, va, va!

RIGOLETTO: And where, if a chance occurs?

SPARAFUCILE: Always here in the evening.

RIGOLETTO: Go away.

SPARAFUCILE: Sparafucile, Sparafucile.

RIGOLETTO: Go away, go away, go away, go away.

SPARAFUCILE *leaves.* RIGOLETTO *watches him go.*

RIGOLETTO: Pari siamo! io la lingua, egli ha il pugnale; l'uomo son io che ride, ei quel che spegne! Quel vecchio maledivami! O uomini! o natura! vil, scellerato mi faceste voi! Oh rabbia! esser difforme! oh rabbia! esser buffone! Non dover, non poter altro che ridere! Il retaggio d'ogni uom m'è tolto, il pianto! Questo padrone mio, giovin, giocondo, sì possente, bello, sonnecchiando mi dice: Fa ch'io rida, buffone ... forzarmi deggio e farlo! Oh dannazione! Odio a voi, cortigiani schernitori! Quanta in mordervi ho gioia! Se iniquo son, per cagion vostra è solo. Ma in altr'uomo qui mi cangio! Quel vecchio maledivami! ... Tal pensiero perchè conturba ognor la mente mia? Mi coglierà sventura? Ah no! è follia!

RIGOLETTO: We're the same! I have my tongue, he his dagger; I'm the man that mocks, he the one that kills! That old man cursed me! O mankind! o nature! It is you who have made me vile and wicked! Oh fury! to be deformed! oh fury! to be a clown! I must not, I cannot do anything but joke! Sorrow, every man's heritage, is forbidden to me! That master of mine, young, gay, so powerful, handsome, indolently he tells me: Make me laugh, clown ... and I must force myself to do it! Oh damnation! I hate you, jeering courtiers! How much pleasure I have in needling you! If I am evil, it's your doing alone. But here I change myself into another man! That old man cursed me! ... Why does that thought constantly disturb my mind? Am I going to have bad luck? Ah no! That's foolish!

GILDA *comes out of the house and throws herself into* RIGOLETTO'S *arms.*

RIGOLETTO: Figlia!	RIGOLETTO: Daughter!
GILDA: Mio padre!	GILDA: My father!
RIGOLETTO: A te d'appresso trova sol gioia il core oppresso.	RIGOLETTO: Near you, my heavy heart finds its only joy.
GILDA: Oh quanto amore!	GILDA: Oh, how much love!
RIGOLETTO: Mia vita sei!	RIGOLETTO: You are my life!
GILDA: Oh quanto amore!	GILDA: Oh, how much love!
RIGOLETTO: Senza te in terra qual bene avrei!	RIGOLETTO: Without you, what good would the earth hold for me!
GILDA: Oh quanto amore!	GILDA: Oh, how much love!
{ RIGOLETTO: O figlia mia!	{ RIGOLETTO: O my daughter!
{ GILDA: Padre mio!	{ GILDA: My father!
GILDA: Voi sospirate! Che v'ange tanto? Lo dite a questa povera figlia ... Se v'ha mistero per lei sia franto ... Ch'ella conosca la sua famiglia.	GILDA: You're sighing! What troubles you so much? Tell it to this poor daughter ... If there is some secret, let it be revealed for her sake ... Let her know her family.
RIGOLETTO: Tu non ne hai.	RIGOLETTO: You have none.
GILDA: Qual nome avete?	GILDA: What is your name?
RIGOLETTO: A te che importa?	RIGOLETTO: What does it matter to you?
GILDA: Se non volete di voi parlarmi—	GILDA: If you don't want to speak to me of yourself—
RIGOLETTO *(interrupting)*: Non uscir mai—	RIGOLETTO *(interrupting)*: Don't ever go out—
GILDA: Non vo che al tempio.	GILDA: The only place I go is to church.
RIGOLETTO: Oh ben tu fai.	RIGOLETTO: Oh, you do right, then.

GILDA: Se non di voi, almen chi sia fate ch'io sappia la madre mia.

GILDA: If not about yourself, at least let me learn about my mother.

RIGOLETTO: Ah! Deh non parlare al misero del suo perduto bene ... Ella sentia, quell'angelo, pietà delle mie pene. Solo, difforme, povero, per compassion mi amò. Ah! morìa, morìa ... le zolle coprano lievi quel capo amato. Sola or tu resti, sola or tu resti al misero. Dio sii ringraziato, sii ringraziato!

RIGOLETTO: Ah! don't speak to a sorrowing man of his bygone happiness ... She took pity, that angel, on my suffering. Out of pity she loved me, alone, deformed, poor. Ah! She died, she died . . . may the earth lightly cover that beloved head. You alone remain, you alone remain to the unhappy man. God be thanked, be thanked!

GILDA: Oh quanto dolor! quanto dolor! che spremere sì amaro pianto può?

GILDA: Oh, how much sorrow! how much sorrow! What can squeeze out such bitter tears?

GILDA: Quanto dolor! quanto dolor! che spremere sì amaro pianto può? Padre, non più, padre, non più, padre, non più, non più, calmatevi, mi lacera tal vista, non più, vi calmate, non più, mio padre, ah vi calmate, padre, mi lacera, padre, mi lacera tal vista, padre, non più, padre, non più, padre, non più, non più, calmatevi, mi lacera tal vista, non più, vi calmate, non più, mio padre, ah vi calmate, padre, mi lacera, padre, mi lacera tal vista!

GILDA: How much sorrow! how much sorrow! What can squeeze out such bitter tears? Father, no more, father, no more, father, no more, no more, calm yourself, such a sight wounds me, no more, calm yourself, no more, my father, ah, calm yourself, father, such a sight wounds me, father, wounds me, father, no more, father, no more, father, no more, no more, calm yourself, such a sight wounds me, no more, calm yourself, no more, my father, ah, calm yourself, father, such a sight wounds me, father, wounds me, father!

RIGOLETTO: Tu sola, sola resti al misero, sola, ah sì, tu sola resti al misero, sola resti al misero, sola tu resti. Dio, sii ringraziato, ringraziato, ah sì, tu sola resti al misero, sola resti al misero, sola tu resti. Dio, sii ringraziato, ringraziato!

RIGOLETTO: You alone, alone remain to the unhappy man, alone, ah yes, you alone remain to the unhappy man, you alone remain to the unhappy man, you alone remain. God be thanked, thanked, ah yes, you alone remain to the unhappy man, alone remain to the unhappy man, you alone remain. God be thanked, thanked!

GILDA: Il nome vostro ditemi, il duol che sì v'attrista.

GILDA: Tell me your name, the pain that so grieves you.

RIGOLETTO: A che nomarmi? È inutile! Padre ti sono, e basti. Me forse al mondo temono, d'alcuno ho forse gli asti ... Altri mi maledicono.

RIGOLETTO: Why name myself? It's useless! I'm your father, and that's enough. Perhaps the world dreads me, perhaps someone bears me a grudge ... Others curse me.

GILDA: Patria, parenti, amici voi dunque non avete?

GILDA: Haven't you then a homeland, family, friends?

RIGOLETTO: Patria! parenti! amici! Culto, famiglia, la patria, il mio universo, il mio universo è in te!

RIGOLETTO: Homeland! family! friends! Religion, family, homeland, my universe, my universe is in you!

GILDA: Ah, se può lieto rendervi, gioia è la vita, la vita a me!

GILDA: Ah, if I can make you happy, life, life is a joy to me!

RIGOLETTO: Culto, famiglia, la patria, il mio universo, il mio universo è in te! Il mio universo è in te!

GILDA: Ah, se può lieto, può lieto rendervi, gioia è la vita, la vita a me! Gioia, gioia è la vita a me!

RIGOLETTO: Religion, family, homeland, my universe, my universe is in you! My universe is in you!

GILDA: Ah, if I can make you happy, can make you happy, life, life is a joy to me! Life is a joy, a joy to me!

GILDA: Già da tre lune son qui venuta, nè la cittade ho ancor veduta; se il concedete, farlo or potrei—	GILDA: It's already three months since I came here, and I have not yet seen the city; couldn't you allow me to do that now—
RIGOLETTO: Mai, mai! Uscita, dimmi, unqua sei?	RIGOLETTO: Never, never! Tell me, have you ever gone out?
GILDA: No.	GILDA: No.
RIGOLETTO: Guai!	RIGOLETTO: Look out!
GILDA *(aside)*: (Ah! che dissi!)	GILDA *(aside)*: (Ah! what did I say!)
RIGOLETTO: Ben te ne guarda! *(Aside:)* (Potrien seguirla, rapirla ancora! Qui d'un buffone si disonora la figlia e se ne ride ... Orror!) Olà?	RIGOLETTO: Be very careful about it! *(Aside:)* (They could follow her, seize her as well! They dishonor a jester's daughter here and laugh about it ... Horror!) Hey there?
GIOVANNA *(coming from the house)*: Signor?	GIOVANNA *(coming from the house)*: Sir?
RIGOLETTO: Venendo, mi vide alcuno? Bada, di' il vero.	RIGOLETTO: Did anyone see me arriving? Take care, tell the truth.
GIOVANNA: Ah no, nessuno.	GIOVANNA: Ah, no, no one.
RIGOLETTO: Sta ben. La porta che dà al bastione è sempre chiusa?	RIGOLETTO: Good. The door that opens to the wall, is it always closed?
GIOVANNA: Ognor si sta, ognor si sta, ognor si sta.	GIOVANNA: It always is, it always is, it always is.
RIGOLETTO: Bada, di' il ver, bada, di' il ver.	RIGOLETTO: Take care, tell the truth, take care, tell the truth.
RIGOLETTO: Ah! veglia, o donna, questo fiore che a te puro confidai; veglia attenta, e non sia mai che s'offuschi il suo candor. Tu dei venti dal furore, ch'altri fiori hanno piegato, lo difendi, e immacolato lo ridona al genitor.	RIGOLETTO: Ah! woman, protect this pure flower that I entrusted to you; protect it closely, and don't ever let its innocence grow dim. Defend it from the raging winds which have bent other flowers, and return it unscathed to her father.

GILDA: Quanto affetto! quali cure! che temete, padre mio? Lassù in cielo, presso Dio, veglia un angiol protettor. Da noi toglie le sventure di mia madre il priego santo; non fia mai disvelto o franto questo a voi diletto fior.

GILDA: How much affection! such cares! What do you fear, my father? Up there in heaven, next to God, a guardian angel watches. My mother's holy prayers will keep misfortunes from us; this flower you love will never be uprooted or broken.

RIGOLETTO: Ah! veglia, o donna, questo fiorc che a te puro confi— Alcun v'è fuori . . .

RIGOLETTO: Ah! woman, protect this pure flower that I en— There's someone outside . . .

RIGOLETTO *opens the door of the courtyard; while he is outside in the street, the* DUKE *slips inside the courtyard and, tossing a purse to* GIOVANNA, *hides behind a tree.*

GILDA: Cielo! Sempre novel sospetto.

RIGOLETTO *(returning and addressing* GIOVANNA*)*: Alla chiesa vi seguiva mai nessuno?

GIOVANNA: Mai.

DUKE: (Rigoletto!)

RIGOLETTO: Se talor qui picchian, guardatevi d'aprire.

GIOVANNA: Nemmeno al Duca?

RIGOLETTO: Non che ad altri a lui! Mia figlia,—

RIGOLETTO: —addio.

DUKE: (Sua figlia!)

GILDA: Addio, mio padre.

GILDA: Heavens! Always a new suspicion.

RIGOLETTO *(returning and addressing* GIOVANNA*)*: No one has ever followed you to church?

GIOVANNA: Never.

DUKE: (Rigoletto!)

RIGOLETTO: If anyone ever knocks here, beware against opening.

GIOVANNA: Not even to the Duke?

RIGOLETTO: Not to him of all others! My daughter,—

RIGOLETTO: —farewell.

DUKE: (His daughter!)

GILDA: Farewell, my father.

RIGOLETTO: Ah! veglia, o donna, questo fiore che a te puro confidai; veglia attenta e non sia mai che s'offuschi il suo candor. Tu dei venti dal furore ch'altri fiori hanno piegato, lo difendi, e immacolato lo ridona al genitor. Ah! veglia, o donna, ah! veglia, o donna, questo fior, ah! veglia, o donna, ah! veglia, o donna, questo fior, ah! veglia, o donna, questo fior, veglia, o donna, questo fior, ah! veglia, o donna, questo fior, veglia, o donna, questo fior, veglia, o donna, veglia, o donna, questo fior!

GILDA: Oh quanto affetto! quali cure! che temete, che temete, padre mio? Lassù in cielo, presso Dio, veglia un angiol protettor, lassù in ciel, lassù in ciel, lassù in ciel, lassù in ciel, lassù in cielo, lassù in cielo, presso Dio, veglia un angiol protettor, in cielo, presso Dio, in cielo, presso Dio, in cielo veglia, veglia un angiol protettor, in cielo, presso Dio, in cielo, presso Dio, in cielo veglia, veglia un angiol protettor, lassù in cielo, presso Dio, veglia un angiol protettor, lassù in cielo, presso Dio, veglia un angiol protettor, lassù in cielo veglia un angiol protettor.

RIGOLETTO: Ah! woman, protect this pure flower that I entrusted to you; protect it closely, and don't ever let its innocence grow dim. Defend it from the raging winds which have bent other flowers, and return it unscathed to her father. Ah! Woman, protect, woman, protect this flower, ah! Woman, protect, woman, protect this flower, ah! Woman, protect this flower, woman, protect this flower, ah! Woman, protect this flower, woman, protect this flower, woman, protect, woman, protect this flower!

GILDA: Oh, how much affection! such cares! What do you fear, what do you fear, my father? Up there in heaven, next to God, a guardian angel watches, up there in heaven, up there in heaven, up there in heaven, up there in heaven, up there in heaven, up there in heaven, next to God, a guardian angel watches, in heaven, next to God, in heaven, next to God, in heaven he watches, a guardian angel watches, in heaven, next to God, in heaven, next to God, in heaven a guardian angel watches, watches, up there in heaven, next to God, a guardian angel watches, up there in heaven, next to God, a guardian angel watches, up there in heaven a guardian angel watches.

RIGOLETTO: Figlia, mia figlia, addio! GILDA: Padre, mio padre, addio!	RIGOLETTO: Daughter, my daughter, farewell! GILDA: Father, my father, farewell!

GILDA *and* RIGOLETTO *embrace.* RIGOLETTO *goes out, closing the door behind him.*

GILDA: Giovanna, ho dei rimorsi.	GILDA: Giovanna, I have pangs of guilt.
GIOVANNA: E perchè mai?	GIOVANNA: And why?
GILDA: Tacqui che un giovin ne seguiva al tempio.	GILDA: I did not say that a young man has been following us to church.
GIOVANNA: Perchè ciò dirgli? L'odiate dunque cotesto giovin, voi?	GIOVANNA: Why tell him that? Do you hate that young man, then?
GILDA: No, no, chè troppo è bello e spira amore.	GILDA: No, no, he's too handsome and inspires love.
GIOVANNA: E magnanimo sembra . . . e gran signore.	GIOVANNA: And he seems generous . . . and a grand gentleman.
GILDA: Signor nè principe io lo vorrei; sento che povero, sento che povero più l'amerei. Sognando o vigile sempre lo chiamo, e l'alma in estasi le dice t'a—	GILDA: I would not wish him to be a gentleman or a prince; I think that poor, I think that poor I'd love him more. Dreaming or waking I constantly call him, and my ecstatic soul tells him: I l—

The DUKE *comes out of hiding, signals* GIOVANNA *to leave them and, falling on his knees before* GILDA, *completes her sentence.*

DUKE: T'amo! T'amo! Ripetilo, sì caro accento, un puro schiudimi ciel di contento!	DUKE: I love you! I love you! Repeat it, that word so dear, open a heaven of pure bliss to me!

GILDA: Giovanna? Giovanna? Ahi misera! non v'è più alcuno che qui rispondami! Oh Dio! nessuno!

GILDA: Giovanna? Giovanna? Ah, woe! There is no longer anyone here to answer me! Oh God! no one!

DUKE: Son io coll'anima che ti rispondo. Ah due che s'amano son tutto un mondo!

DUKE: It's I that answer you with my soul. Ah, two who love each other are a whole world!

GILDA: Chi mai, chi giungere vi fece a me?

GILDA: Who ever, who ever let you come to me?

DUKE: Se angelo o demone, che importa a te? Io t'amo ...

DUKE: Whether angel or demon, what does it matter to you? I love you ...

GILDA: Uscitene.

GILDA: Go away from here.

DUKE: Uscire! adesso! Ora che accendene un fuoco istesso! Ah, inseparabile d'amore il Dio stringeva, o vergine, tuo fato al mio! È il sol dell'anima, la vita è amore, sua voce è il palpito del nostro core; e fama e gloria, potenza e trono, umane fragili qui cose sono; una pur avvene, sola, divina, è amor che agl'angeli, agl'angeli più ne avvicina! Adunque amiamoci, donna celeste, d'invidia agl'uomini sarò per te, d'invidia agl'uomini sarò per te.

DUKE: Go away! at this moment! Now that the same fire is burning in us! Ah, the god of love has bound your fate inseparably to mine, O maiden! Love is the soul's sunlight, it is life, its voice is our heartbeat; and fame and glory, power and throne are fragile mortal things here; there is only one divine thing, it's love, which brings us nearer to the angels, to the angels! Then let us love each other, heavenly woman, you'll make me the envy of mankind, you'll make me the envy of mankind!

GILDA: Ah, de' miei vergini sogni son queste le voci tenere, sì care a me! Son queste le voci, le voci tenere, sì care, sì

GILDA: Ah, these are the tender words of my maiden dreams, so dear to me! These are the words, the tender words, so

care a me! Ah, de' miei sogni, ah sì, son queste le voci tenere, sì care a me! Ah, de' miei sogni, ah sì, son queste le voci tenere, sì care a me! A me! ah! care a me, ah! sì care a me!

dear, so dear to me! Ah, these are the tender words of my dreams, ah, yes, so dear to me! Ah, these are the tender words of my dreams, ah yes, so dear to me! To me! ah! dear to me, ah! so dear to me!

DUKE: Amiamoci, amiamoci, d'invidia agl'uomini sarò per te, d'invidia agl'uomini sarò per te! Adunque amiamoci, donna celeste, d'invidia agl'uomini sarò per te! per te! ah! per te! ah! ah sì, per te!

DUKE: Let us love each other, let us love each other, you'll make me the envy of mankind, you'll make me the envy of mankind! Then let us love each other, heavenly woman, you'll make me the envy of mankind! You will! ah! You will! ah! Ah, yes, you will!

DUKE: Che m'ami, deh! ripetimi . . .

DUKE: That you love me, come! tell me again . . .

GILDA: L'udiste.

GILDA: You heard it.

DUKE: Oh me felice!

DUKE: Oh, happy me!

GILDA: Il nome vostro ditemi; saperlo non mi lice?

GILDA: Telll me your name; am I not allowed to know it?

CEPRANO *(to* BORSA, *in the street)*: Il loco è qui—

CEPRANO *(to* BORSA, *in the street)*: Here's the place—

DUKE *(thinking)*: Mi nomino—

DUKE *(thinking)*: My name is—

BORSA *(to* CEPRANO*)*: Sta ben!

BORSA *(to* CEPRANO*)*: Good!

DUKE: —Gualtier Maldè—studente sono—e povero.

DUKE: —Walter Maldé—I'm a student—and poor.

GIOVANNA *(returning, frightened)*: Rumor di passi è fuori—

GIOVANNA *(returning, frightened)*: There's a sound of footsteps outside—

GILDA: Forse mio padre—

GILDA: Perhaps my father—

DUKE: (Ah, cogliere potessi il traditore che sì mi sturba!)

DUKE: (Ah, if I could catch the traitor who's interrupting me like this!)

GILDA *(to* GIOVANNA*)*: Adducilo di qua al bastione—

GILDA: —or ite.

DUKE: Di': M'amerai tu?

GILDA: E voi?

DUKE: L'intera vita—poi—

GILDA: Non più ... non più ... partite ... non più ... partite ...

DUKE: Addio, addio, speranza ed anima.

GILDA: Addio, addio, speranza ed anima.

DUKE: Sol tu sarai, sarai per me. Sol tu sarai, sarai per me!

GILDA: Sol tu sarai, sarai per me, sarai per me!

DUKE: Addio, addio—

GILDA: Addio, addio—

DUKE: Addio—

DUKE & GILDA: Addio ... vivrà, vivrà, vivrà immutabile l'affetto mio per te, per te, sì, vivrà, vivrà, vivrà immutabile l'affetto mio per te, vivrà immutabile l'affetto mio per te, per te.

DUKE: Addio.

GILDA: Addio.

DUKE: Addio.

GILDA: Addio.

DUKE & GILDA: Speranza sola sarai per me.

GILDA *(to* GIOVANNA*)*: Take him from here to the wall—

GILDA: —go now.

DUKE: Speak: You'll love me?

GILDA: And you?

DUKE: All my life—then—

GILDA: No more ... no more ... depart ... no more ... depart ...

DUKE: Farewell, farewell, hope and soul.

GILDA: Farewell, farewell, hope and soul.

DUKE: You alone will exist, exist for me. You alone will exist, exist for me!

GILDA: You alone will exist, exist for me, exist for me!

DUKE: Farewell, farewell—

GILDA: Farewell, farewell—

DUKE: Farewell—

DUKE & GILDA: Farewell ... my love for you will live, will live, will live unchangingly, for you, yes, my love for you will live, will live, will live unchangingly, my love for you, for you will live unchangingly.

DUKE: Farewell.

GILDA: Farewell.

DUKE: Farewell.

GILDA: Farewell.

DUKE & GILDA: You will be all my hope.

DUKE: Addio.

GILDA: Addio.

DUKE: Addio.

GILDA: Addio.

DUKE & GILDA: Speranza sola sarai per me.

GILDA: Addio.

DUKE: Addio.

GILDA: Addio.

DUKE: Addio.

GILDA: Addio.

DUKE: Addio.

GILDA & DUKE: Addio! Addio!

DUKE: Farewell.

GILDA: Farewell.

DUKE: Farewell.

GILDA: Farewell.

DUKE & GILDA: You will be all my hope.

GILDA: Farewell.

DUKE: Farewell.

GILDA: Farewell.

DUKE: Farewell.

GILDA: Farewell.

DUKE: Farewell.

GILDA & DUKE: Farewell, farewell!

The DUKE *goes into the house, escorted by* GIOVANNA. GILDA *remains, looking at the door through which he has just gone.*

GILDA: Gualtier Maldè! nome di lui sì amato, ti scolpisci nel core innamorato! Caro nome che il mio cor festi primo palpitar, le delizie dell'amor mi dêi sempre rammentar! Col pensier il mio desir a te sempre volerà, e fin l'ultimo sospir, caro nome, tuo sarà! Col pensier il mio desir a te sempre volerà, e fin l'ultimo mio sospir, caro nome, tuo sarà! Col pensier il mio desir a te sempre volerà, a te volerà, fin l'ultimo sospir, fin l'ultimo sospir, caro nome, tuo sarà, caro nome, tuo sarà. Il mio

GILDA: Walter Maldé! Name of him so beloved, you are engraved in my adoring heart! Dear name that first caused my heart to throb, you shall always remind me of love's delights! My longing thoughts will always fly to you, and until my final breath, dear name, they'll be of you! My longing thoughts will always fly to you, and until my final breath, dear name, they'll be of you! My longing thoughts will always fly to you, fly to you, until my final breath, until my final breath, dear name, they'll

desir a te ognora volerà, fin l'ultimo sospiro tuo sarà. *(She mounts to the terrace with a lantern in her hand.)* Gualtier Maldè! Gualtier Maldè! caro nome che il mio cor festi primo palpitar—

be of you, dear name, they'll be of you. My longing will fly to you forever, it will be for you until my final breath. *(She mounts to the terrace with a lantern in her hand.)* Walter Maldé! Walter Maldé! dear name that first caused my heart to throb—

MARULLO, CEPRANO, BORSA *and courtiers, armed and masked, appear in the street.* GILDA'S *voice grows fainter as she enters the house.*

BORSA *(pointing out* GILDA *to the others)*: È là.

GILDA: —e fin l'ultimo sospir—

CEPRANO: Miratela.

CHORUS: Oh, quanto è bella!

GILDA: —caro nome, tuo sarà.

MARULLO: Par fata od angiol.

GILDA: Gualtier Maldè! Gualtier Maldè!

CHORUS: L'amante è quella di Rigoletto!

BORSA, MARULLO, CEPRANO, CHORUS: Oh! quanto è bella!

BORSA *(pointing out* GILDA *to the others)*: There she is.

GILDA: —and until my final breath—

CEPRANO: Look at her.

CHORUS: Oh, how beautiful she is!

GILDA: —they'll be of you.

MARULLO: She looks like a fairy or an angel.

GILDA: Walter Maldé! Walter Maldé!

CHORUS: That is Rigoletto's beloved!

BORSA, MARULLO, CEPRANO, CHORUS: Oh! How beautiful she is!

Enter RIGOLETTO, *thinking.*

RIGOLETTO: Riedo! perchè?

RIGOLETTO: I'm back! What for?

BORSA: Silenzio ... all'opra ... badate a me.

BORSA: Quiet ... let's get to it ... pay attention to me.

RIGOLETTO: (Ah, da quel vecchio fui maledetto!) *(Colliding with* BORSA:*)* Chi va là?

RIGOLETTO: (Ah, I was cursed by that old man!) *(Colliding with* BORSA:*)* Who goes there?

BORSA *(to courtiers)*: Tacete ... c'è Rigoletto.

BORSA *(to courtiers)*: Be still ... it's Rigoletto.

CEPRANO: Vittoria doppia! l'uccideremo.

CEPRANO: A double victory! Let's kill him.

BORSA: No, che domani più rideremo.

BORSA: No, for we'll laugh the more tomorrow.

MARULLO: Or tutto aggiusto ...

MARULLO: Now I'll get everything ready ...

RIGOLETTO: Chi parla qua?

RIGOLETTO: Who's speaking there?

MARULLO: Ehi! Rigoletto ... Di' ...

MARULLO: Hey! Rigoletto ... Say ...

RIGOLETTO *(in a wild tone of voice)*: Chi va là?

RIGOLETTO *(in a wild tone of voice)*: Who goes there?

MARULLO: Eh non mangiarci! Son—

MARULLO: Eh, don't bite us. I'm—

RIGOLETTO: Chi?

RIGOLETTO: Who?

MARULLO: Marullo.

MARULLO: Marullo.

RIGOLETTO: In tanto buio lo sguardo è nullo.

RIGOLETTO: I can't make out anything in such darkness.

MARULLO: Qui ne condusse ridevol cosa; torre a Ceprano vogliam la sposa.

MARULLO: A ludicrous thing brought us here; we want to steal Ceprano's wife.

RIGOLETTO: (Ahimè, respiro!) Ma come entrare?

RIGOLETTO: (Ah me, I breathe again!) But how to get in?

MARULLO *(to* CEPRANO*)*: (La vostra chiave?) *(To* RIGOLETTO:*)* Non dubitare. Non dee mancarci lo stratagemma. Ecco la chiave. *(He gives the key to* RIGOLETTO.*)*

MARULLO *(to* CEPRANO*)*: (Your key?) *(to* RIGOLETTO:*)* Don't worry. We won't lack the means. Here's the key. *(He gives the key to* RIGOLETTO.*)*

RIGOLETTO *(feeling the key)*: Sento il suo stemma. *(Aside:)* (Ah, terror vano fu dunque il mio.) *(To the courtiers:)* N'è là il palazzo. Con voi son io.

RIGOLETTO *(feeling the key)*: I feel its crest. *(Aside:)* (Ah. my fear was in vain, then.) *(To the courtiers:)* His palace is there. I'm with you.

MARULLO: Siam mascherati.

MARULLO: We're masked.

RIGOLETTO: Ch'io pur mi mascheri; a me una larva.

RIGOLETTO: Let me be masked, too; give me a disguise.

MARULLO: Sì, pronta è già. Terrai la scala.

MARULLO: Yes, here's one all ready. You will hold the ladder.

He puts a mask on RIGOLETTO, *at the same time tying a handkerchief over it. He then leads* RIGOLETTO *to hold the ladder which has been placed against the terrace.*

RIGOLETTO: Fitta è la tenebra.

RIGOLETTO: The darkness is thick.

MARULLO *(to courtiers)*: La benda cieco e sordo il fa.

MARULLO *(to courtiers)*: The blindfold makes him blind and deaf.

BORSA, MARULLO, CEPRANO, CHORUS: Zitti, zitti, moviamo a vendetta, ne sia colto or che men l'aspetta. Derisore sì audace, costante a sua volta schernito sarà! Cheti, cheti, rubiamgli l'amante, e la corte doman riderà. Cheti, cheti, rubiamgli l'amante, e la corte doman riderà.

BORSA, MARULLO, CEPRANO, CHORUS: Softly, softly, let's get revenge, let him be trapped now that he least expects it. A mocker so brazen and constant, he'll be scorned in his turn! Quietly, quietly, let us steal his beloved from him, and tomorrow the court will laugh. Quietly, quietly, let us steal his beloved from him, and tomorrow the court will laugh.

Some of the courtiers climb to the terrace, force a window, and enter. They then open the street door to admit the others.

BORSA, MARULLO, CEPRANO, CHORUS: Cheti, cheti, cheti, cheti, cheti, cheti, cheti, cheti, cheti, cheti, rubiamgli l'amante, e la corte doman riderà, cheti, cheti, rubiamgli l'amante, e la corte doman riderà. Derisore sì audace, sì audace e costante, derisore sì audace, a sua volta schernito sarà! Derisore sì audace, sì audace e costante, derisore sì audace. a sua volta schernito sarà!

CEPRANO, BASSES: Zitti, zitti, zitti, zitti, cheti, cheti, cheti, cheti, zitti, zitti, zitti, zitti,—

BORSA, MARULLO, TENORS: Zitti, cheti, zitti, cheti, cheti, cheti,—

BORSA, MARULLO, CEPRANO, CHORUS: —cheti, attenti all'opra, all'opra, all'opra, attenti, attenti all'opra.

BORSA, MARULLO, CEPRANO, CHORUS: Quietly, quietly, quietly, quietly, quietly, quietly, quietly, quietly, quietly, quietly, let us steal his beloved from him, and tomorrow the court will laugh. Quietly, quietly, let us steal his beloved from him, and tomorrow the court will laugh. A mocker so brazen, so brazen and constant, a mocker so brazen, he'll be scorned in his turn! A mocker so brazen, so brazen and constant, a mocker so brazen, he'll be scorned in his turn!

CEPRANO, BASSES: Softly, softly, softly, softly, quietly, quietly, quietly, quietly, softly, softly, softly, softly,—

BORSA, MARULLO, TENORS: Softly, quietly, softly, quietly, quietly, quietly,—

BORSA, MARULLO, CEPRANO, CHORUS: —quietly, pay attention to the job, to the job, to the job, pay attention, pay attention to the job.

They drag GILDA *out of the house, a handkerchief tied over her mouth. As she is borne across the stage, she loses a scarf.*

GILDA *(from afar)*: Soccorso, padre mio!

BORSA, MARULLO, CEPRANO, CHORUS: Vittoria!

GILDA *(from afar)*: Help, my father!

BORSA, MARULLO, CEPRANO, CHORUS: Victory!

GILDA *(from farther away)*: Aita!

GILDA *(from farther away)*: Help!

RIGOLETTO *(touching his eyes)*: Non han finito ancor! Qual derisione! Sono bendato!

RIGOLETTO *(touching his eyes)*: Aren't they done yet? What a joke! I'm blindfolded!

He snatches off the blindfold and the mask. Seizing a lantern left behind by one of the courtiers, he notices GILDA's *scarf; terrified, he rushes into the house and drags out* GIOVANNA. *After several attempts, he is finally able to speak.*

RIGOLETTO: Ah! ah! ah! La maledizione! *(He collapses.)*

RIGOLETTO: Ah! ah! ah! The curse! *(He collapses.)*

ACT THREE

ACT THREE

A room in the DUKE's *palace. Doors at the rear and on both sides. Portraits of the* DUKE *and Duchess on the walls. A table, an armchair and other furniture. The* DUKE *enters, agitated.*

DUKE: Ella mi fu rapita! E quando, o ciel? Ne' brevi istanti, prima che il mio presagio interno sull'orma corsa ancora mi spingesse! Schiuso era l'uscio! e la magion deserta! E dove ora sarà quell'angiol caro? colei che prima potè in questo core destar la fiamma di costanti affetti? colei sì pura, al cui modesto sguardo quasi spinto a virtù talor mi credo! Ella mi fu rapita! E chi l'ardiva? Ma ne avrò, ma ne avrò vendetta: lo chiede il pianto della mia diletta. Parmi veder le lagrime scorrenti da quel ciglio, quando fra il dubbio e l'ansia del subito periglio, dell'amor nostro memore, dell'amor nostro memore, il suo Gualtier chiamò. Ned ei potea soccorerti, cara fanciulla amata; ei che vorria dell'anima farti quaggiù beata; ei che le

DUKE: She was snatched from me! And when, o heaven? In the brief moments before my inner foreboding made me rush back again! The door was open! and the dwelling deserted! And where can that dear angel be now? She that first could kindle the flame of steadfast love in this heart? She so pure, at whose modest glance I believed myself almost turned virtuous? She was snatched from me! And who dared to do it? But I'll have, but I'll have revenge for it: My beloved's tears demand it. I seem to see the tears flowing from those eyes, when between the worry and fear of imminent danger, remembering our love, remembering our love, she called for her Walter. He was unable to help you, dear beloved maiden; he that from

sfere agl'angeli, ei che le sfere agl'angeli per te non invidiò, ei che le sfere, le sfere agl'angeli per te, per te, le sfere agl'angeli per te non invidiò, non, non invidiò per te!

his soul wants to make you happy on earth; he that didn't envy the heavenly angels, the heavenly angels for your sake, the heavenly angels, the heavenly angels, the heavenly angels he didn't envy, no, he didn't envy for your sake, for your sake, for your sake, for your sake!

Enter MARULLO, BORSA, CEPRANO *and other courtiers.*

MARULLO, BORSA, CEPRANO, CHORUS: Duca, Duca!

MARULLO, BORSA, CEPRANO, CHORUS: Duke, Duke!

DUKE: Ebben?

DUKE: Well?

MARULLO, BORSA, CEPRANO, CHORUS: L'amante fu rapita a Rigoletto!

MARULLO, BORSA, CEPRANO, CHORUS: Rigoletto's girlfriend has been taken!

DUKE: Come? e donde?

DUKE: How? and where?

MARULLO, BORSA, CEPRANO, CHORUS: Dal suo tetto!

MARULLO, BORSA, CEPRANO, CHORUS: From his house!

DUKE: Ah, ah! Dite, come fu? Dite, dite, come fu? *(He sits.)*

DUKE: Ha, ha! Tell, how was it? Tell, tell, how was it? *(He sits.)*

BORSA, MARULLO, CEPRANO, CHORUS: Scorrendo uniti remota via, brev'ora dopo caduto il dì, come previsto ben s'era in pria, rara beltà—

BORSA, MARULLO, CEPRANO, CHORUS: Moving together through a distant street, a short time after nightfall, as we expected right from the first, we discovered—

BORSA, TENORS: —ci si scoprì.

BORSA, TENORS: —an exquisite beauty there.

MARULLO, CEPRANO, BASSES: —ci si scoprì.

MARULLO, CEPRANO, BASSES: —an exquisite beauty there.

BORSA, MARULLO, CEPRANO, CHORUS: Era l'amante di Rigoletto, che, vista appena, si dile-

BORSA, MARULLO, CEPRANO, CHORUS: It was Rigoletto's beloved, who vanished as soon

guò. Già di rapirla, s'avea il progetto, quando il buffon—

as we saw her. We had just planned to seize her, when the jester—

BORSA, TENORS: —ver noi spuntò;—

BORSA, TENORS: —came toward us.

MARULLO, CEPRANO, BASSES: —ver noi spuntò;—

MARULLO, CEPRANO, BASSES: —came toward us.

BORSA, MARULLO, CEPRANO, CHORUS: —che di Ceprano noi la contessa rapir volessimo, stolto credè; la scala quindi all'uopo messa, bendato, ei stesso ferma tenè, la scala quindi ei stesso, ei stesso ferma, ferma tenè. Salimmo, e rapidi la giovinetta a noi riusciva quindi asportar.

BORSA, MARULLO, CEPRANO, CHORUS: The fool believed that we wanted to seize Ceprano's countess; so, blindfolded, he himself held steady the ladder that had been placed there for the purpose, so he himself, he himself, held the ladder, held it steady. We climbed, and quickly succeeded in carrying off the young woman.

DUKE *(aside)*: (Cielo!)

DUKE *(aside)*: (Heaven!)

BORSA, MARULLO, CEPRANO, CHORUS: Quand'ei s'accorse della vendetta—

BORSA, MARULLO, CEPRANO, CHORUS: When he became aware of our revenge—

DUKE: (È dessa! la mia diletta!)

DUKE: (It's my beloved herself!)

MARULLO, CEPRANO, CHORUS: —restò scornato ad imprecar, ad imprecar—

MARULLO, CEPRANO, CHORUS: —he remained, dishonored, to curse, to curse—

BORSA, MARULLO, CEPRANO, CHORUS: —restò scornato ad imprecar, restò scornato ad imprecare, restò scornato ad imprecar, restò scornato ad imprecar, restò scornato ad imprecare, restò scornato ad imprecar,—

BORSA, MARULLO, CEPRANO, CHORUS: —he remained, dishonored, to curse, he remained, dishonored, to curse, he remained, dishonored, to curse, he remained, dishonored, to curse, he remained, dishonored, to curse, he remained, dishonored, to curse—

BORSA, TENORS: —ad imprecar,—

BORSA, TENORS: —to curse,—

MARULLO, TENORS: —ad imprecar,—

MARULLO, TENORS: —to curse,—

BORSA, MARULLO, CEPRANO, CHORUS: —restò scornato ad imprecar,—

BORSA, MARULLO, CEPRANO, CHORUS: —he remained, dishonored, to curse,—

BORSA, TENORS: —ad imprecar,—

BORSA, TENORS: —to curse,—

MARULLO, TENORS: —ad imprecar,—

MARULLO, TENORS: —to curse,—

BORSA, MARULLO, CEPRANO, CHORUS: —restò scornato ad imprecar, ad imprecar, ad imprecar, ad imprecar, ad imprecar!

BORSA, MARULLO, CEPRANO, CHORUS: —he remained, dishonored, to curse, to curse, to curse, to curse, to curse!

DUKE *(to courtiers)*: Ma dove or trovasi la poveretta?

DUKE *(to courtiers)*: But where is the poor girl now?

BORSA, MARULLO, CEPRANO, CHORUS: Fu da noi stessi addotta or qui.

BORSA, MARULLO, CEPRANO, CHORUS: We ourselves brought her here.

DUKE *(aside)*: (Ah, tutto il ciel non mi rapì!) *(He makes a motion of joy.)* Possente amor mi chiama, volar io deggio a lei; il serto mio darei per consolar quel cor, il serto mio darei per consolar quel cor. Ah! sappia alfin chi l'ama, conosca alfin chi sono, apprenda ch'anco in trono ha degli schiavi Amor, apprenda ch'anco in trono, ch'anco in trono ha degli schiavi, ha degli schiavi Amor.

DUKE *(aside)*: (Ah, heaven didn't take everything from me!) *(He makes a motion of joy.)* Powerful love is calling me, I must fly to her; I'd give my coronet in order to comfort that heart, I'd give my coronet in order to comfort that heart. Ah! finally she'll know who loves her, finally she'll know who I am, she'll learn that Love has some slaves even on thrones, she'll learn that Love has some slaves, has some slaves even on thrones, even on thrones.

MARULLO, CEPRANO, BORSA, CHORUS: Oh qual pensier or l'agita, or l'agita? come cangiò d'umor, come cangiò d'umor! oh qual pensier or l'agita? come cangiò d'umor! oh qual pensier or l'agita, quale pensier or l'agita? come cangiò d'umor! come cangiò, come cangiò!

MARULLO, CEPRANO, BORSA, CHORUS: Oh, what intention moves him now, moves him now? How his mood has changed, how his mood has changed! Oh, what intention moves him now? How his mood has changed! Oh, what intention moves him now, what intention moves him now? How his mood has changed! How it has changed, how it has changed!

DUKE: Ah! Possente amor mi chiama, volar io deggio a lei, il serto mio darei per consolar quel cor, il serto mio darei per consolar quel cor. Ah, sappia alfin chi l'ama, conosca alfin chi sono, apprenda ch'anco in trono ha degli schiavi Amor, apprenda ch'anco in trono, ch'anco in trono ha degli schiavi, ha degli schiavi Amor—

DUKE: Ah! Powerful love is calling me, I must fly to her, I'd give my coronet in order to comfort that heart, I'd give my coronet in order to comfort that heart. Ah, finally she'll know who loves her, finally she'll know who I am, she'll learn that Love has some slaves even on thrones, she'll learn that even on thrones, even on thrones he has some slaves, Love has some slaves—

MARULLO, CEPRANO, BORSA, CHORUS: Oh, qual pensiero l'agita, oh, qual pensiero l'agita? Come cangiò d'umor—

MARULLO, CEPRANO, BORSA, CHORUS: Oh, what intention moves him, oh, what intention moves him? How his mood has changed!

DUKE: —ha degli schiavi Amor—

MARULLO, CEPRANO, BORSA, CHORUS: —come cangiò, come cangiò d'umor!

DUKE: —Love has some slaves—

MARULLO, CEPRANO, BORSA, CHORUS: —how his mood has changed, how it's changed!

MARULLO, CEPRANO, BORSA, CHORUS: Oh, qual pensiero l'agita, oh, qual pensiero l'agita? Come cangiò d'umor—

DUKE: —ha degli schiavi Amor, ha degli schiavi Amor, ha degli schiavi Amor, Amor!

MARULLO, CEPRANO, BORSA, CHORUS: —come cangiò, come cangiò d'umor!

MARULLO, CEPRANO, BASSES: —come cangiò—

BORSA, TENORS: —come cangiò d'umor!

MARULLO, CEPRANO, BASSES: —cangiò d'umor! come cangiò, cangiò d'umor!—

BORSA, TENORS: —come cangiò d'umor!

MARULLO, CEPRANO, BORSA, CHORUS: —come cangiò, cangiò d'umor!

MARULLO, CEPRANO, BORSA, CHORUS: Oh, what intention moves him, oh, what intention moves him? How his mood has changed—

DUKE: —Love has some slaves, Love has some slaves, Love, Love has some slaves!

MARULLO, CEPRANO, BORSA, CHORUS: —how it's changed, how his mood has changed!

MARULLO, CEPRANO, BASSES: —how it's changed—

BORSA, TENORS: —how his mood has changed!

MARULLO, CEPRANO, BASSES: —his mood has changed! How his mood has changed, has changed!—

BORSA, TENORS: —How his mood has changed!

MARULLO, CEPRANO, BORSA, CHORUS: —How it's changed, how his mood has changed!

The DUKE *goes out hastily through the center door. As the courtiers talk to one another,* RIGOLETTO *is heard offstage. He enters with restrained sorrow.*

MARULLO: Povero Rigoletto!

RIGOLETTO: La rà, la rà, la la, la rà, la rà, la rà, la rà—

CHORUS: Ei vien! Silenzio.

RIGOLETTO: —la rà, la rà, la la, la rà, la rà.

MARULLO: Poor Rigoletto!

RIGOLETTO: La ra, la ra, la la, la ra, la ra, la ra, la ra—

CHORUS: He's coming! Quiet.

RIGOLETTO: —la ra, la ra, la la, la ra, la ra.

BORSA, MARULLO, CEPRANO, CHORUS: Oh buon giorno, Rigoletto.

RIGOLETTO *(aside)*: (Han tutti fatto il colpo!)

CEPRANO: Ch'hai di nuovo, buffon?

RIGOLETTO *(mimicking)*: Ch'hai di nuovo, buffon? Che dell'usato più noioso voi siete.

BORSA, MARULLO, CEPRANO, CHORUS *(laughing)*: Ah! ah! ah!

RIGOLETTO *(restlessly looking all about)*: La rà, la rà, la la, la rà, la rà, la rà, la rà. (Ove l'avran nascosta?)

BORSA, MARULLO, CEPRANO, CHORUS *(among themselves)*: Guardate com'è inquieto!

RIGOLETTO: La rà, la rà, la rà, la rà, la rà, la rà, la la,—

RIGOLETTO: —la rà, la rà, la rà, la la.

BORSA, MARULLO, CEPRANO, CHORUS: Sì! sì guardate com'è inquieto!

RIGOLETTO *(to* MARULLO*)*: Son felice che nulla a voi nuocesse l'aria di questa notte.

MARULLO: Questa notte!

RIGOLETTO: Sì ... Oh fu il bel colpo—

MARULLO: S'ho dormito sempre.

BORSA, MARULLO, CEPRANO, CHORUS: Oh, good morning, Rigoletto.

RIGOLETTO *(aside)*: (They all were in on it!)

CEPRANO: What news do you have, clown?

RIGOLETTO *(mimicking)*: What news do you have, clown? That you're more tiresome than usual.

BORSA, MARULLO, CEPRANO, CHORUS *(laughing)*: Ha! ha! ha!

RIGOLETTO *(restlessly looking all about)*: La ra, la ra, la la, la ra, la ra, la ra, la ra. (Where have they hidden her?)

BORSA, MARULLO, CEPRANO, CHORUS *(among themselves)*: Look how uneasy he is!

RIGOLETTO: La ra, la ra, la ra, la ra, la ra, la ra, la la,—

RIGOLETTO: —la ra, la ra, la ra, la la.

BORSA, MARULLO, CEPRANO, CHORUS: Yes! yes! Look how uneasy he is!

RIGOLETTO *(to* MARULLO*)*: I'm glad that last night's air did you no harm.

MARULLO: Last night!

RIGOLETTO: Yes ... Oh, it was a lovely prank—

MARULLO: I slept throughout.

RIGOLETTO: Ah, voi dormiste! Avrò dunque sognato!

RIGOLETTO: Ah, you slept! Then I was dreaming!

He withdraws and, seeing a handkerchief on a table, looks at it uneasily and hides it.

RIGOLETTO: La rà, la rà, la rà, la rà, la rà, la rà, la la.

RIGOLETTO: La ra, la ra, la ra, la ra, la ra, la ra, la la.

BORSA, MARULLO, CEPRANO, CHORUS: (Ve', ve', come tutto osserva!)

BORSA, MARULLO, CEPRANO, CHORUS: (See, see, how he's looking at everything!)

RIGOLETTO *(throwing it down)*: (Non è il suo.) Dorme il Duca tuttor?

RIGOLETTO *(throwing it down)*: (It isn't hers.) Is the Duke still asleep?

BORSA, MARULLO, CEPRANO, CHORUS: Sì, dorme ancora.

BORSA, MARULLO, CEPRANO, CHORUS: Yes, he's still sleeping.

One of the Duchess's pages enters.

PAGE: Al suo sposo parlar vuol la Duchessa.

PAGE: The Duchess would like to speak to her husband.

CEPRANO: Dorme.

CEPRANO: He's sleeping.

PAGE: Qui or or con voi non era?

PAGE: Wasn't he here with you just now?

BORSA: È a caccia.

BORSA: He's at the hunt.

PAGE: Senza paggi! Senz'armi!

PAGE: Without pages! Without weapons!

BORSA, MARULLO, CEPRANO, CHORUS: E non capisci che per ora vedere non può alcuno?

BORSA, MARULLO, CEPRANO, CHORUS: And don't you understand that he can't see anyone just now?

RIGOLETTO, *who has been listening attentively to this conversation, suddenly leaps between them and interrupts.*

RIGOLETTO: Ah, ella è qui dunque! Ella è col Duca!

BORSA, MARULLO, CEPRANO, CHORUS: Chi?

RIGOLETTO: La giovin che stanotte al mio tetto rapiste ... Ma la saprò riprender ... Ella è là ...

BORSA, MARULLO, CEPRANO, CHORUS: Se l'amante perdesti, la ricerca altrove.

RIGOLETTO: Io vo' mia figlia ...

BORSA, MARULLO, CEPRANO, CHORUS: La sua figlia!

RIGOLETTO: Sì, la mia figlia—D'una tal vittoria—che? adesso non ridete?

RIGOLETTO: Ah, then she's here! She's with the Duke!

BORSA, MARULLO, CEPRANO, CHORUS: Who?

RIGOLETTO: The young person whom you took from my house last night ... But I'll get her back! ... She's there ...

BORSA, MARULLO, CEPRANO, CHORUS: If you've lost your mistress, look for her somewhere else.

RIGOLETTO: I want my daughter ...

BORSA, MARULLO, CEPRANO, CHORUS: His daughter!

RIGOLETTO: Yes, my daughter—What? Aren't you laughing now at such a triumph?

He runs toward one of the doors, but the courtiers bar his way.

RIGOLETTO: Ella è là! la voglio ... la renderete! Cortigiani, vil razza dannata, per qual prezzo vendeste il mio bene? A voi nulla per l'oro sconviene! Ma mia figlia è impagabil tesor. La rendete ... o, se pur disarmata, questa man per voi fora cruenta; nulla in terra più l'uomo paventa, se dei figli difende l'onor.

RIGOLETTO: She's there! I want her ... give her back! Courtiers, damned evil race, what price did you sell my darling for? You find nothing too vile for gold! But my daughter is a priceless treasure. Give her back ... or even weaponless, this hand will be covered with your blood; a man has nothing more to fear on earth if he defends his children's honor.

He again throws himself at the door, and the courtiers again bar his way. Miserably, he comes to the front of the stage.

RIGOLETTO: Quella porta, assassini, assassini, m'aprite, la porta, la porta, assassini, m'aprite! Ah! voi tutti a me contro venite! tutti contro me! Ah! Ebben—piango ... Marullo, signore, tu ch'hai l'alma gentil come il core, dimmi tu dove l'hanno nascosta? Marullo ... signore, dimmi tu dove l'hanno nascosta? È là? Non è vero? È là? Non è vero? È là? Non è vero? Tu taci! ohimè! *(Weeping:)* Miei signori, perdono, pietate—al vegliardo la figlia ridate! Ridonarla a voi nulla ora costa, a voi nulla ora costa, tutto, tutto al mondo è tal figlia per me. Signori, perdon, perdono, pietà; ridate a me la figlia; tutto al mondo è tal figlia per me. Ridate a me la figlia; tutto al mondo ell'è per me! Pietà, pietà, signori, pietà, signori, pietà!

RIGOLETTO: Open that door for me, murderers, murderers, open that door, that door for me, murderers, open it! Ah! You're all against me! all against me! Well, then—I'll weep ... Marullo, sir, you whose soul is as kind as your heart, tell me where they've hidden her? Marullo ... sir, tell me where they've hidden her? She's there? Isn't it so? She's there? Isn't it so? She's there? Isn't it so? You're silent! woe is me! *(Weeping:)* My lords, pardon, have pity—give an old man back his daughter! It will cost you nothing to give her back now, it will cost you nothing now, that daughter is everything, everything in the world to me. Sirs, pardon, pardon, have pity; give me back my daughter; that daughter is everything in the world to me. Give me back my daughter; she's everything in the world to me! Have pity, have pity, sirs, have pity, sirs, have pity!

GILDA *runs out of one of the side rooms and throws herself into* RIGOLETTO'S *arms.*

GILDA: Mio padre!

GILDA: My father!

RIGOLETTO: Dio! mia Gilda! Signori—in essa è tutta la mia famiglia ... *(To* GILDA:*)* Non

RIGOLETTO: God! my Gilda! My lords—in her is my whole family ... *(To* GILDA:*)* Don't temer più nulla, angelo mio ... *(To courtiers:)* —fu scherzo! non è vero? Io che pur piansi or rido. *(To* GILDA:*)* E tu, a che piangi?

be afraid of anything any more, my angel ... *(To courtiers:)* It was a joke! Isn't that so? I who was just weeping now laugh. *(To* GILDA:*)* And you, what are you weeping about?

GILDA: Ah! l'onta, padre mio!

GILDA: Ah! the shame, my father!

RIGOLETTO: Cielo! che dici?

RIGOLETTO: Heavens! What are you saying?

GILDA: Arrossir voglio innanzi a voi soltanto.

GILDA: I want to save my blushes for you alone.

RIGOLETTO *(turning toward the courtiers in an imperious way)*: Ite di qua, voi tutti. Se il Duca vostro d'appressarsi osasse, ch'ei non entri, gli dite, e ch'io ci sono. *(He throws himself on a chair.)*

RIGOLETTO *(turning toward the courtiers in an imperious way)*: Get out of here, all of you. If your Duke dares to approach, tell him not to enter, and that I am here. *(He throws himself on a chair.)*

BORSA, MARULLO, CEPRANO, CHORUS *(to themselves)*: Coi fanciulli e co' dementi, spesso giova il simular. Partiam pur, ma quel ch'ei tenti non lasciamo d'osservar. *(They leave, closing the door behind them.)*

BORSA, MARULLO, CEPRANO, CHORUS *(to themselves)*: With children and with madmen, it's often useful to pretend. Let's leave, then, but let's not stop watching whatever he's doing. *(They leave, closing the door behind them.)*

RIGOLETTO: Parla, siam soli.

RIGOLETTO: Speak, we're alone.

GILDA: (Ciel! dammi coraggio!) Tutte le feste al tempio mentre pregava Iddio, bello e fatale un giovine offriasi al guardo mio. Se i labbri nostri tacquero, dagl'occhi il cor, il cor parlò. Furtivo fra le tenebre sol ieri a me giungeva: Sono studente

GILDA: (Heaven! Give me courage!) Every holy day at church, while I was praying to God, a handsome young man would inevitably come to my notice. If our lips kept silent, our hearts, our hearts spoke through our eyes. Only yes-

povero, commosso mi diceva, e con ardente palpito amor mi protestò. Partì ... partì ... il mio core aprivasi a speme più gradita, quando improvvisi apparvero color che m'han rapita, e a forza qui m'addussero nell' ansia più crudel.

terday, hidden among the shadows, he followed me. "I'm a poor student," he movingly said to me, and ardently declared his burning love. He left ... he left ... my heart swelled with the most welcome hope, when suddenly appeared those men who seized me and by force brought me here, suffering cruel anxiety.

RIGOLETTO *(aside)*: (Ah! Solo per me l'infamia a te chiedeva, o Dio— ch'ella potesse ascendere quanto caduto er'io. Ah! presso del patibolo bisogna ben l'altare! Ma tutto, ma tutto ora scompare—l'altare si rovesciò! Tutto scompare—l'altar si rovesciò!) Ah! *(To* GILDA:*)* Piangi, piangi, fanciulla, fanciulla, piangi!

RIGOLETTO *(aside)*: (Ah! I asked you for disgrace for myself alone, o God, that she might be able to climb as far as I have fallen. Ah! An altar is needed most next to the gallows! But everything, everything now vanishes—the altar is overturned. Everything vanishes—the altar is overturned!) Ah! *(To* GILDA:*)* Weep, weep, child, child, weep.

GILDA: Padre!

GILDA: Father!

RIGOLETTO: Scorrer, scorrer fa il pianto sul mio cor.

RIGOLETTO: Let your tears flow, flow on my heart.

GILDA: Padre, in voi parla un angel per me consolator.

GILDA: Father, an angel speaks through you to comfort me.

RIGOLETTO: Piangi, piangi, fanciulla, fanciulla, piangi, scorrer, scorrer fa il pianto sul mio cor. Piangi, piangi, piangi, scorrer fa il pianto sul mio cor. Piangi, piangi, piangi, scorrer fa il pianto sul mio cor, fa il pianto sul mio cor, fa il pianto

RIGOLETTO: Weep, weep, child, child, weep, let your tears flow, flow on my heart. Weep, weep, weep, let your tears flow on my heart. Weep, weep, weep, let your tears flow on my heart, weep on my heart, weep on my heart, ah! on my heart, ah! Let

sul mio cor, ah! ah! sul mio cor, ah! scorrer fa il pianto, mia figlia, mia figlia, sul mio cor.

your tears flow, my daughter, my daughter, on my heart.

GILDA: Padre, in voi parla un angel, padre, in voi parla un angel, padre, in voi parla un angel consolator. Padre, in voi parla un angel consolator, angel consolator, angel consolator, ah! consolator, ah! padre, in voi un angel, un angel consolator.

GILDA: Father, an angel speaks through you, father, an angel speaks through you, father, a comforting angel speaks through you. Father, a comforting angel speaks through you, a comforting angel, comforting angel, ah! comforting, ah! father, an angel through you, a comforting angel.

RIGOLETTO: Compiuto pur quanto a fare mi resta, lasciare potremo quest'aura funesta.

RIGOLETTO: Once I finish what I still have to do, we'll be able to leave this dreadful place.

GILDA: Sì.

GILDA: Yes.

RIGOLETTO *(aside)*: (E tutto un sol giorno cangiare potè!)

RIGOLETTO *(aside)*: (And only one day could change everything!)

An usher enters, followed by MONTERONE, *who crosses the stage, guarded by halberdiers.*

USHER: Schiudete—ire al carcere Monteron dee.

USHER: Make way—Monterone must go to prison.

MONTERONE *(halting before the* DUKE's *portrait)*: Poichè fosti invano da me maledetto, nè un fulmine o un ferro colpiva il tuo petto, felice pur anco, o Duca, vivrai . . .

MONTERONE *(halting before the* DUKE's *portrait)*: Since my curse upon you was in vain, and neither a thunderbolt nor a sword has pierced your breast, you'll go on living happily, o Duke . . .

Exit MONTERONE *and the guards.*

RIGOLETTO: No, vecchio, t'inganni—un vindice avrai. Sì, vendetta, tremenda vendetta di quest'anima è solo desio. Di punirti già l'ora s'affretta, che fatale per te tuonerà. Come fulmin scagliato da Dio, come fulmin scagliato da Dio, te colpire il buffone saprà.

RIGOLETTO: No, old man, you're wrong—you'll be avenged. Yes, vengeance, terrible vengeance is my soul's only wish. It's already drawing near, the hour of your punishment that will fatally burst forth on you. Like a thunderbolt hurled by God, like a thunderbolt hurled by God, your jester will strike you.

GILDA: O mio padre, qual gioia feroce balenarvi negl'occhi vegg'io!

GILDA: O my father, what fierce joy do I see gleaming in your eyes!

RIGOLETTO: Vendetta!

RIGOLETTO: Vengeance!

GILDA: Perdonate, a noi pure una voce di perdono dal cielo verrà—

GILDA: Forgive, even to us a voice of forgiveness will come from heaven—

RIGOLETTO: Vendetta!

RIGOLETTO: Vengeance!

GILDA: —perdonate—

GILDA: —forgive—

RIGOLETTO: No!

RIGOLETTO: No!

GILDA: —perdonate!

GILDA: —forgive!

RIGOLETTO: No!

RIGOLETTO: No!

GILDA: (Mi tradiva, pur l'amo, gran Dio! Per l'ingrato ti chiedo pietà.)

GILDA: (He betrayed me, yet I love him, great God! I ask your pity for the thankless wretch!)

RIGOLETTO: Come fulmin scagliato da Dio,—

RIGOLETTO: Like a thunderbolt hurled by God,—

GILDA: Perdonate—

GILDA: Forgive—

RIGOLETTO: —te colpire il buffon saprà,—

RIGOLETTO: —your jester will strike you,—

RIGOLETTO: —colpire te il buffone, te colpire saprà, colpire il buffone, te colpire saprà, sì, sì,

RIGOLETTO: —your jester will strike you, strike you, your jester will strike you, strike you, colpire, te colpire il buffone saprà!

GILDA: A noi pure il perdono dal ciel verrà, a noi pure il perdono dal ciel verrà, a noi verrà, ah, perdonate, perdonate!

yes, yes, your jester will strike, strike you!

GILDA: Even to us forgiveness will come from heaven, even to us forgiveness will come from heaven, will come to us, ah, forgive, forgive!

They go out together.

ACT FOUR

ACT FOUR

It is night at a deserted spot near the banks of the Mincio River. The audience can see the inside of a decrepit two-story inn, where SPARAFUCILE *sits at a table. Outside the inn—unseen by* SPARAFUCILE, *but clearly visible to the audience—*RIGOLETTO *and* GILDA *wait agitatedly.*

RIGOLETTO: E l'ami?	RIGOLETTO: And you love him?
GILDA: Sempre.	GILDA: Always.
RIGOLETTO: Pure tempo a guarirne t'ho lasciato.	RIGOLETTO: And yet I've given you time to cure yourself of that.
GILDA: Io l'amo!	GILDA: I love him!
RIGOLETTO: Povero cor di donna! Ah il vile infame! Ma ne avrai vendetta, o Gilda.	RIGOLETTO: Pathetic heart of womankind! Ah, the vile scoundrel! But you'll be avenged for it, Gilda.
GILDA: Pietà, mio padre!	GILDA: Have mercy, my father!
RIGOLETTO: E se tu certa fossi ch'ei ti tradisse, l'ameresti ancora?	RIGOLETTO: And if you were certain that he was betraying you, would you still love him?
GILDA: Nol sò—ma pur m'adora.	GILDA: I don't know—but then he loves me.
RIGOLETTO: Egli?	RIGOLETTO: He?
GILDA: Sì.	GILDA: Yes.

RIGOLETTO *leads her closer to the house, indicating that she should watch through a crack in the wall.*

RIGOLETTO: Ebben, osserva dunque.

GILDA: Un uomo vedo.

RIGOLETTO: Per poco attendi.

RIGOLETTO: Ah well, watch, then.

GILDA: I see a man.

RIGOLETTO: Listen for a bit.

The DUKE, *dressed as a cavalry officer, enters the inn.*

GILDA *(surprised)*: Ah padre mio!

DUKE *(to* SPARAFUCILE*)*: Due cosc, c tosto

SPARAFUCILE: Quali?

DUKE: Una stanza e del vino—

RIGOLETTO: (Son questi i suoi costumi!)

SPARAFUCILE: (Oh il bel zerbino!)

GILDA *(surprised)*: Ah, father!

DUKE *(to* SPARAFUCILE*)*: Two things, and right away—

SPARAFUCILE: What?

DUKE: A room and some wine.

RIGOLETTO: (Those are his practices.)

SPARAFUCILE: (Oh, the handsome dandy!)

SPARAFUCILE *goes into an adjoining room.*

DUKE: La donna è mobile qual piuma al vento, muta d'accento e di pensiero. Sempre un amabile leggiadro viso, in pianto o in riso, è menzognero. La donna è mobil qual piuma al vento, muta d'accento e di pensier, e di pensier, e, e di pensier. È sempre misero chi a lei s'affida, chi le confida mal cauto il core! Pur mai non sentesi felice appieno chi su quel seno non liba amore! La donna è mobil qual piuma al vento, muta d'accento e di pensier, e di pensier, e, e di pensier!

DUKE: Woman is fickle as a feather in the breeze, changeable in word and in thought. A comely, lovable face, weeping or smiling, it's always deceitful. Woman is fickle as a feather in the breeze, changeable in word and in thought, and in thought, and, and in thought. He's always pitiable, he who entrusts to her his poorly guarded heart! Yet he's never felt complete happiness whose heart hasn't imbibed love! Woman is fickle as a feather in the breeze, changeable in word and in thought, and in thought, and, and in thought!

SPARAFUCILE *returns with a bottle of wine and two glasses, which he sets on the table; then he raps twice on the ceiling with the hilt of his long sword. At this signal, a smiling young woman in gypsy dress bounds down the stairs. The* DUKE *runs to embrace her, but she evades him.* SPARAFUCILE *goes outside and speaks to* RIGOLETTO.

SPARAFUCILE: È là il vostr'-uomo—Viver dee o morire?

SPARAFUCILE: There's your man. Should he live or die?

RIGOLETTO: Più tardi tornerò l'opra a compire.

RIGOLETTO: I'll come back later to finish the job.

SPARAFUCILE *goes off, behind the house and along the river. From the street,* RIGOLETTO *and* GILDA *continue looking inside the inn.*

DUKE: Un dì, se ben rammentomi, o bella, t'incontrai. Mi piacque di te chiedere, e intesi che qui stai. Or sappi, che d'allora sol te quest'alma adora.

DUKE: One day, if I remember rightly, I met you, pretty girl. It suited me to ask about you, and I found out you live here. Now you must know that since that time my soul has loved only you.

GILDA: Iniquo!

GILDA: Wicked man!

MADDALENA: Ah, ah, e vent'altre appresso le scorda forse adesso? Ha un'aria il signorino da vero libertino!

MADDALENA: Ha, ha, aren't you now perhaps forgetting the nearly twenty others? The young gentleman has an air of the true libertine!

DUKE *(embracing her)*: Sì! un mostro son—

DUKE *(embracing her)*: Yes! I'm a monster!—

GILDA: Ah padre mio!
MADDALENA: Lasciatemi, stordito.

GILDA: Ah, father!
MADDALENA: Leave me be, madcap.

DUKE: Ih, che fracasso!

DUKE: Ugh, what a fuss!

MADDALENA: Stia saggio.

MADDALENA: Be sensible.

DUKE: E tu sii docile, non fare tanto chiasso. Ogni saggezza chiudesi nel gaudio e nell'amore. *(Taking* MADDALENA'S *hand:)* La bella mano candida!

MADDALENA: Scherzate voi, signore.

DUKE: No, no.

MADDALENA: Son brutta.

DUKE: Abbracciami.

GILDA: Iniquo!

MADDALENA: Ebro!

DUKE *(laughing)*: D'amor ardente.

MADDALENA: Signor l'indifferente, vi piace canzonar?

DUKE: No, no, ti vo' sposar.

MADDALENA: Ne voglio la parola—

DUKE *(with irony)*: Amabile figluola!

RIGOLETTO *(to* GILDA*)*: E non ti basta ancor?

GILDA: Iniquo traditor!

MADDALENA: Ne voglio la parola!

DUKE: Amabile figluola!

RIGOLETTO: E non ti basta ancor?

GILDA: Iniquo traditor!

MADDALENA: Ne voglio la parola!

DUKE: And you calm down, don't make such a racket. All wisdom is contained in mirth and love. *(Taking* MADDALENA'S *hand:)* Your lovely white hand!

MADDALENA: You're joking, sir.

DUKE: No, no.

MADDALENA: I'm ugly.

DUKE: Embrace me.

GILDA: Wicked man!

MADDALENA: Lunatic!

DUKE *(laughing)*: Burning with love.

MADDALENA: Carefree sir, do you like telling fibs?

DUKE: No, no, I want to marry you.

MADDALENA: I want your word for it—

DUKE *(with irony)*: Lovable wench!

RIGOLETTO *(to* GILDA*)*: And haven't you had enough yet?

GILDA: Wicked betrayer!

MADDALENA: I want your word for it!

DUKE: Lovable wench!

RIGOLETTO: And haven't you had enough yet?

GILDA: Wicked betrayer!

MADDALENA: I want your word for it!

MADDALENA: Ne voglio la parola, ne voglio la parola!

DUKE: Amabile figluola! amabile figluola!

RIGOLETTO: E non ti basta ancor? E non ti basta ancor?

DUKE: Bella figlia dell'amore, schiavo son de' vezzi tuoi; con un detto, un detto sol tu puoi le mie pene, le mie pene consolar. Vieni e senti del mio core il frequente palpitar. Con un detto, un detto sol tu puoi le mie pene, le mie pene consolar.

MADDALENA: Ah! ah! rido ben di core, chè tai baie costan poco;—

GILDA: Ah! così parlar d'amore.

MADDALENA: —quanto valga il vostro gioco, mel credete, sò apprezzar.

GILDA: —a me pur l'infame ho udito!

RIGOLETTO *(to* GILDA*)*: Taci, il piangere non vale;—

GILDA: Infelice cor tradito, per angoscia non scoppiar, no, no, non scoppiar.

DUKE: Con un detto sol tu puoi le mie pene consolar.

MADDALENA: Son avvezza, bel signore, ad un simile scherzare, mio bel signor!

MADDALENA: I want your word for it, I want your word for it!

DUKE: Lovable wench! lovable wench!

RIGOLETTO: And haven't you had enough yet? And haven't you had enough yet?

DUKE: Love's pretty daughter, I'm a slave to your charms; with a word, just a word, you could comfort my pangs, my pangs. Come and feel the rapid beating of my heart. With a word, with just a word, you could comfort my pangs, my pangs.

MADDALENA: Ha, ha! I'm laughing heartily, for such jokes cost so little.

GILDA: Ah! to speak like that about love.

MADDALENA: You'd better believe that I know how to take your fooling at its worth.

GILDA: I've listened to the liar myself!

RIGOLETTO *(to* GILDA*)*: Be quiet, it's useless to cry.

GILDA: Unhappy betrayed heart, don't burst with anguish, no, no, don't burst.

DUKE: With just a word you could comfort my pangs.

MADDALENA: I'm used, handsome sir, to banter like this, my handsome sir!

RIGOLETTO: —taci, taci, il piangere non vale, no, non val, no, no, non val.

RIGOLETTO: Be quiet, be quiet, it's useless to cry, no, no, it's no use, no, no, it's no use.

DUKE: Bella figlia dell'amore,—

DUKE: Love's pretty daughter,—

DUKE: —schiavo son de' vezzi tuoi; con un detto, un detto sol tu puoi le mie pene, le mie pene consolar. Ah! con un detto sol tu puoi le mie pene consolar; vieni e senti del mio core il frequente palpitar, ah, sì, vieni; ah! con un detto sol tu puoi le mie pene consolar; vieni e senti del mio core il frequente palpitar, ah, sì, vieni, senti del core il palpitar, senti del core il palpitar, vieni, vieni, vieni, vieni!

DUKE: —I'm a slave to your charms; with a word, just a word, you could comfort my pangs, my pangs. Ah! With just a word, you could comfort my pangs; come and feel the rapid beating of my heart, ah yes, come; ah! with just a word, you could comfort my pangs; come and feel the rapid beating of my heart, ah, yes, come, feel the beating of my heart, feel the beating of my heart, come, come, come, come!

GILDA: Infelice cor tradito, ah! no, non scoppiar. Infelice core, cor tradito, per angoscia non scoppiare, infelice cor tradito, per angoscia non scoppiare, infelice cor tradito, per angoscia non scoppiar, no, no, no, no, no, no, no, non scoppiare, infelice cor tradito, per angoscia non scoppiare, infelice cor tradito, per angoscia non scoppiare, infelice cor tradito, per angoscia non scoppiar, no, no, no, no, no, no, no, non scoppiar, infelice cor tradito, per angoscia non scoppiar, infelice cor tradito, per angoscia non

GILDA: Unhappy betrayed heart, ah! No, don't burst. Unhappy heart, betrayed heart, don't burst with anguish, unhappy betrayed heart, don't burst with anguish, unhappy betrayed heart, don't burst with anguish, no, no, no, no, no, no, no, don't burst, unhappy betrayed heart, don't burst with anguish, unhappy betrayed heart, don't burst with anguish, unhappy betrayed heart, don't burst with anguish, no, no, no, no, no, no, no, don't burst, unhappy betrayed heart, don't burst with

scoppiar, no, non scoppiar, non scoppiar, ah no!*

MADDALENA: Ah! ah! rido ben di core, chè tai baie costan poco; quanto valga il vostro gioco, mel credete, sò apprezzar. Sono avvezza, bel signore, ad un simile scherzare. Ah! ah! ah! ah! rido di cor, ah, ah, rido di cor, ah! ah! rido di cor, ah, ah, rido, ah! ah! rido ben di core, chè tai baie costan poco; quanto valga il vostro gioco, mel credete, sò apprezzar, sì, sì, sono avvezza, bel signore, ad un simile scherzar, ah, ah, ah, ah! rido di cor, ah! ah! rido di cor, ah! ah! rido di cor, ah! ah! rido, ah! ah! rido ben di core, chè tai baie costan poco; quanto valga il vostro gioco, mel credete, sò apprezzar, sì, sì, sono avvezza, bel signore, ad un simile scherzar, il vostro gioco sò apprezzar, il vostro gioco sò apprezzar, il vostro gioco sò apprezzare, ah sì!

anguish, unhappy betrayed heart, don't burst with anguish, no, don't burst, no, don't burst, ah, no!

MADDALENA: Ha! ha! I'm laughing heartily, for such jokes cost so little; you'd better believe that I know how to take your fooling at its worth. I'm used, handsome sir, to banter like this. Ha! ha! ha! ha! I'm laughing heartily, ha, ha, I'm laughing heartily, ha! ha! I'm laughing heartily, ha, ha, I'm laughing, ha! ha! I'm laughing heartily, for such jokes cost so little; you'd better believe that I know how to take your fooling at its worth, yes, yes, I'm used, handsome sir, to banter like this; ha, ha, ha, ha! I'm laughing heartily, ha! ha! I'm laughing heartily, ha! ha! I'm laughing heartily, ha! ha! I'm laughing, ha! ha! I'm laughing heartily, for such jokes cost so little; you'd better believe that I know how to take your fooling at its worth, yes, yes, I'm used, handsome sir, to banter like this, I know how to take your fooling at its worth, I know how to take your fooling at its worth, I know how to take your fooling at its worth, I

* In some versions, GILDA's last words in the quartet are: "Perchè, o credulo mio core, un tal uom dovevi amar!" ("Why, o my credulous heart, did you have to love such a man!").

RIGOLETTO: Ch'ei mentiva, ch'ei mentiva sei sicura. Taci, e mia sarà la cura la vendetta d'affrettar, taci, e mia sarà la cura la vendetta d'affrettar. Sì, pronta fia, sarà fatale, io saprollo fulminar, io saprollo fulminar; taci, e mia sarà la cura la vendetta d'affrettar, taci, e mia sarà la cura la vendetta d'affrettar; sì, pronta fia, sarà fatale, io saprollo fulminar, io saprollo fulminar, taci, e mia sarà la cura la vendetta d'affrettar, taci, e mia sarà la cura la vendetta d'affrettar, taci, taci, taci, taci!

know how to take your fooling at its worth, ah, yes!

RIGOLETTO: You are now assured that he was lying, that he was lying. Be quiet, and I'll take care that vengeance comes soon, be quiet, and I'll take care that vengeance comes soon. Yes, it will be soon, it will be deadly, I will strike him down, I will strike him down; be quiet, and I'll take care that vengeance comes soon, be quiet, and I'll take care that vengeance comes soon; yes, it will be soon, it will be deadly, I will strike him down, I will strike him down, be quiet, and I'll take care that vengeance comes soon, be quiet, and I'll take care that vengeance comes soon, be quiet, be quiet, be quiet, be quiet!

RIGOLETTO *(to* GILDA*)*: M'odi! ritorna a casa ... oro prendi, un destriero, una veste viril che t'apprestai, e per Verona parti; sarovvi io pur doman.

RIGOLETTO *(to* GILDA*)*: Listen! go back home ... take money, a horse, and a suit of men's clothing that I've prepared for you, and leave for Verona; I'll meet you there tomorrow.

GILDA: Or venite.

GILDA: You come now.

RIGOLETTO: Impossibil.

RIGOLETTO: Impossible.

GILDA: Tremo.

GILDA: I'm trembling.

RIGOLETTO: Va!

RIGOLETTO: Go!

GILDA *leaves. Inside the inn, the* DUKE *and* MADDALENA *continue drinking and laughing.* SPARAFUCILE *returns;* RIGOLETTO *counts him out some money.*

RIGOLETTO: Venti scudi hai tu detto? Eccone dieci; e dopo l'opra il resto. Ei qui rimane?

RIGOLETTO: Did you say twenty scudi? Here are ten; the rest after the job. Is he staying here?

SPARAFUCILE: Sì.

SPARAFUCILE: Yes.

RIGOLETTO: Alla mezzanotte ritornerò.

RIGOLETTO: I'll come back at midnight.

SPARAFUCILE: Non cale. A gettarlo nel fiume basto io solo.

SPARAFUCILE: It doesn't matter. I can manage to throw him into the river without help.

RIGOLETTO: No, no, il vo' far io stesso.

RIGOLETTO: No, no, I want to do that myself.

SPARAFUCILE: Sia! Il suo nome?

SPARAFUCILE: So be it! What's his name?

RIGOLETTO: Vuoi saper anche il mio? Egli è *Delitto*, *Punizion* son io.

RIGOLETTO: Do you want to know mine as well? He's *Crime*, I'm *Punishment*.

RIGOLETTO *leaves. The sky darkens and it begins to thunder.*

SPARAFUCILE: La tempesta è vicina! Più scura fia la notte!

SPARAFUCILE: The storm is nearing! The night will be getting darker!

DUKE *(grabbing* MADDALENA*)*: Maddalena!

DUKE *(grabbing* MADDALENA*)*: Maddalena!

MADDALENA *(escaping)*: Aspettate—mio fratello viene.

MADDALENA *(escaping)*: Wait—my brother's coming.

DUKE: Che importa?

DUKE: What does it matter?

MADDALENA: Tuona!

MADDALENA: It's thundering!

SPARAFUCILE *(reentering)*: E pioverà fra poco.

SPARAFUCILE *(reentering)*: And it will rain in a little while.

DUKE: Tanto meglio! *(To* SPARAFUCILE:*)* Tu dormirai in scuderia—all'inferno—ove vorrai!

DUKE: So much the better! *(To* SPARAFUCILE:*)* You'll sleep in the stable—in hell—wherever you want!

SPARAFUCILE: Oh grazie.

MADDALENA *(softly to the* DUKE*)*: (Ah no—partite.)

DUKE *(to* MADDALENA*)*: (Con tal tempo?)

SPARAFUCILE *(aside to* MADDALENA*)*: (Son venti scudi d'oro.) *(To the* DUKE:*)* Ben felice d'offrirvi una stanza; se a voi piace, tosto a vederla andiamo.

SPARAFUCILE: Oh, thanks.

MADDALENA *(softly to the* DUKE*)*: (Ah no—leave.)

DUKE *(to* MADDALENA*)*: (In such weather?)

SPARAFUCILE *(aside to* MADDALENA*)*: (It's twenty golden scudi.) *(To the* DUKE:*)* Very glad to offer you a room; if you like, let's go see it right away.

SPARAFUCILE *takes a light and goes toward the stairs.*

DUKE: Ebben! sono con te ... presto ... vediamo.

DUKE: All right! I'm with you ... quick ... let's see it.

He whispers in MADDALENA'S *ear and follows* SPARAFUCILE.

MADDALENA: Povero giovin! grazioso tanto! *(It thunders again.)* Dio, qual notte è questa!

MADDALENA: Poor young man! so elegant! *(It thunders again.)* God, what a night this is!

In the loft, the DUKE *looks at the unshuttered balcony.*

DUKE: Si dorme all'aria aperta? bene, bene! Buona notte.

SPARAFUCILE: Signor, vi guardi Iddio.

DUKE: Breve sonno dormiam—stanco son io. *(He sings sleepily as he takes off his hat and sword and gets ready to go to bed.)* La donna è mobile qual piuma al

DUKE: Am I supposed to sleep in the open air? All right, all right. Good night.

SPARAFUCILE: Sir, God keep you.

DUKE: Let's sleep a while—I'm tired. *(He sings sleepily as he takes off his hat and sword and gets ready to go to bed.)* Woman is fickle as a feather in the breeze,

vento, muta d'accento e di pensiero ... *(Fading:)* muta d'accento e di pen— la donna è mobil—muta d'accento e di pensier—e di ... pensier ... muta d'accento e di pen—

changeable in word and in thought ... *(Fading:)* changeable in word and in th— Woman is fickle—changeable in word and in thought—and in ... thought ... changeable in word and in th—

He falls asleep. Downstairs, MADDALENA *sits thoughtfully.* SPARAFUCILE *drinks from the bottle left by the* DUKE.

MADDALENA: È amabile in vero cotal giovinotto!

SPARAFUCILE: Oh sì, venti scudi ne dà di prodotto.

MADDALENA: Sol venti? Son pochi! Valeva di più.

SPARAFUCILE: La spada, s'ei dorme, va—portami giù.

MADDALENA: He's really likeable, that young man!

SPARAFUCILE: Oh yes, he's earned us twenty scudi.

MADDALENA: Only twenty? That's little! He was worth more.

SPARAFUCILE: His sword, if he's asleep, go—bring it down to me.

MADDALENA *climbs the stairs to get the* DUKE'S *sword.* GILDA *reenters from the road, dressed as a man with boots and spurs. Slowly she comes toward the inn, where* SPARAFUCILE *continues to drink. The lightning and thunder continue, increasing in intensity.* MADDALENA *comes back downstairs and puts the* DUKE'S *sword on the table.*

GILDA: Ah più non ragiono. Amor mi trascina! Mio padre, perdono. Qual notte d'orrore! Gran Dio, che accadrà!

MADDALENA: Fratello?

GILDA *(looking through the crack into the inn)*: Chi parla?

SPARAFUCILE: Al diavol ten va.

GILDA: Ah, I no longer reason. Love is dragging me! Father, pardon me. What a horrible night! Great God, what is going to happen?

MADDALENA: Brother?

GILDA *(looking through the crack into the inn)*: Who's speaking?

SPARAFUCILE: Go to the devil.

He gets up and begins to grope in a cupboard.

MADDALENA: Somiglia un Apollo quel giovine ... Io l'amo—ei m'ama—riposi—nè più l'uccidiamo!

MADDALENA: That young man looks like an Apollo ... I like him—he likes me—let him sleep—let's not kill him after all!

GILDA *(listening)*: Oh cielo!

GILDA *(listening)*: Oh, heaven!

SPARAFUCILE *tosses a sack to* MADDALENA.

SPARAFUCILE: Rattoppa quel sacco.

SPARAFUCILE: Mend this sack.

MADDALENA: Perchè?

MADDALENA: Why?

SPARAFUCILE: Entr'esso il tuo Apollo, sgozzato da me, gettar dovrò al fiume.

SPARAFUCILE: I intend to throw your Apollo into the river in it, with his throat cut by me.

GILDA: L'inferno qui vedo!

GILDA: I see hell here!

MADDALENA: Eppure il danaro salvarti scommetto, serbandolo in vita.

MADDALENA: Still, I bet I could save the money for you and keep him alive.

SPARAFUCILE: Difficile il credo.

SPARAFUCILE: Hard to believe.

MADDALENA: M'ascolta—anzi facil ti svelo un progetto. De' scudi già dieci dal gobbo ne avesti; venire cogl'altri più tardi il vedrai.

MADDALENA: Listen to me. Not at all, the plan I'll show is simple. You've already received ten scudi from that hunchback; later, you'll see him come with the rest.

MADDALENA: Uccidilo, e venti allora ne avrai—
GILDA: Che sento! mio padre!

MADDALENA: Kill him, and then you'll have twenty—
GILDA: What do I hear! my father!

MADDALENA: —così tutto il prezzo goder si potrà.

MADDALENA: —that way it'll be possible to enjoy the whole price.

SPARAFUCILE: Uccider quel gobbo! che diavol dicesti! Un ladro son forse? Son forse un bandito? Qual altro cliente da me fu tradito? Mi paga quest'uomo, fedele m'avrà.

SPARAFUCILE: Kill that hunchback! What the devil are you saying! Am I perhaps a thief? Am I perhaps a robber? What other customer have I ever double-crossed? That man is paying me, I'll keep my promise to him.

MADDALENA: Ah, grazia per esso.

MADDALENA: Ah, have mercy on this man.

SPARAFUCILE: È duopo ch'ei muoia.

SPARAFUCILE: He must die.

MADDALENA *makes as if to rush upstairs.*

MADDALENA: Fuggire il fo adesso!

MADDALENA: I'll make him run away right now!

GILDA: Oh buona figluola!

GILDA: Oh, good wench!

SPARAFUCILE *(restraining* MADDALENA*)*: Gli scudi perdiamo.

SPARAFUCILE *(restraining* MADDALENA*)*: We'll lose the money.

MADDALENA: È ver!

MADDALENA: It's true!

SPARAFUCILE: Lascia fare.

SPARAFUCILE: Let me go ahead with it.

MADDALENA: Salvarlo dobbiamo, salvarlo dobbiamo.

MADDALENA: We should save him, we should save him.

SPARAFUCILE: Se pria ch'abbia il mezzo la notte toccato alcuno qui giunga, per esso morrà.

SPARAFUCILE: If anyone shows up before the stroke of midnight, he'll die in his place.

MADDALENA: È buia la notte, il ciel troppo irato, nessuno a quest'ora da qui passerà.

MADDALENA: The night is dark, the sky too angry, no one will come by here at this hour.

GILDA: Oh qual tentazione! morir per l'ingrato! Morire, e mio padre! Oh cielo! pietà—

GILDA: Oh, what a temptation! to die for the thankless wretch! To die, and my father! Oh, heaven! Have mercy!—

GILDA: —oh cielo! pietà! oh cielo! pietà! oh cielo! cielo! cielo! pietà!

MADDALENA: È buia la notte, il ciel troppo irato, nessuno a quest'ora da qui passerà, no, no, no, nessuno passerà!

SPARAFUCILE: Se pria ch'abbia il mezzo la notte toccato alcuno qui giunga, per esso morrà, se pria ch'abbia il mezzo la notte toccato alcuno qui giunga, per esso morrà.

GILDA: —Oh heaven! Have mercy! Oh heaven! Have mercy! Oh heaven! heaven! heaven! Have mercy!

MADDALENA: The night is dark, the sky too angry, no one will come by here at this hour, no, no, no, no one will come by!

SPARAFUCILE: If anyone shows up before the stroke of midnight, he'll die in his place, if anyone shows up before the stroke of midnight, he'll die in his place.

First one clock, then another strikes the half hour.

SPARAFUCILE: Ancor c'è mezz'-ora.

MADDALENA: Attendi, fratello.

GILDA: Che! piange tal donna! Nè a lui darò aita! Ah s'egli al mio amore divenne rubello, io vo' per la sua gettar la mia vita.

SPARAFUCILE: There's still a half hour.

MADDALENA: Wait, brother.

GILDA: What! A woman like that weeps, and shall I not come to his aid? Ah, if he's rebelled against my love, I'll lay down my life in exchange for his.

GILDA *knocks at the inn door.*

MADDALENA: Si picchia?

SPARAFUCILE: Fu il vento.

MADDALENA: Is there knocking?

SPARAFUCILE: It was the wind.

The storm continues. GILDA *knocks again.*

MADDALENA: Si picchia, ti dico.

MADDALENA: There's knocking, I tell you.

SPARAFUCILE: È strano! Chi è?

SPARAFUCILE: It's strange! Who is it?

GILDA: Pietà d'un mendico; asil per la notte a lui concedete.

GILDA: Have pity on a beggar; grant him shelter for the night.

MADDALENA: Fia lunga tal notte!

MADDALENA: It will be a long night!

SPARAFUCILE *goes to grope in the cupboard.*

SPARAFUCILE: Alquanto attendete.

SPARAFUCILE: Wait a bit.

MADDALENA: Su spicciati, presto, fa l'opra compita: anelo una vita con altra salvar.

MADDALENA: Come on, hurry up, finish the job: I'm longing to save one life with another.

SPARAFUCILE: Ebbene—son pronto, quell'uscio dischiudi; più ch'altro gli scudi mi preme salvar.

SPARAFUCILE: All right, I'm ready, open that door; more than anything else I'm concerned with saving the scudi.

GILDA: Ah! presso alla morte, sì giovane, sono! Oh ciel, per quegl'empi ti chieggo perdono!

GILDA: Ah! I'm so young to be near death! Oh heaven, I ask your forgiveness for these sinners!

GILDA: Perdona tu, o padre, a quest'infelice! sia l'uomo felice ch'or vado a salvar; perdona, perdona, o padre! perdona! sia l'uomo felice ch'or vado a salvar, sia l'uomo felice ch'or vado a salvar.

GILDA: Your forgiveness, o father, for this unhappy girl! Let the man be happy whom I'm now going to save, forgive me, forgive me, o father! Forgive! Let the man be happy whom I'm now going to save, let the man be happy whom I'm now going to save.

MADDALENA: Spicciati, presto, fa l'opra compita; anelo una vita con altra salvar; su, su, fa presto, su, su, fa presto, su, su, fa presto, su, su, fa presto; anelo una vita con altra salvar,

MADDALENA: Hurry up, quickly, finish the job; I'm longing to save one life with another; come on, come on, be quick, come on, come on, be quick, come on, come on, be quick,

anelo una vita con altra salvar,
anelo una vita con altra salvar.

come on, come on, be quick; I'm longing to save one life with another, I'm longing to save one life with another, I'm longing to save one life with another.

SPARAFUCILE: Bene, son pronto, quell'uscio dischiudi; più ch'altro gli scudi mi preme salvar; ebbene, son pronto, quell'uscio dischiudi; più ch'altro gli scudi mi preme salvar; ebbene, son pronto, quell'uscio dischiudi; più ch'altro gli scudi mi preme salvar; ah sì, gli scudi mi preme salvar, più ch'altro gli scudi mi preme salvar, più ch'altro gli scudi mi preme salvar.

SPARAFUCILE: Well, I'm ready, open that door; more than anything else I'm concerned with saving the scudi; all right, I'm ready, open that door; more than anything else I'm concerned with saving the scudi; all right, I'm ready, open that door; more than anything else I'm concerned with saving the scudi; ah, yes, I'm concerned with saving the scudi; more than anything else I'm concerned with saving the scudi; more than anything else I'm concerned with saving the scudi.

GILDA *knocks again.*

MADDALENA: Spicciati!

SPARAFUCILE: Apri.

MADDALENA: Hurry up!

SPARAFUCILE: Open.

He hides behind the door with his dagger. MADDALENA *opens the door.*

MADDALENA: Entrate.

GILDA: Dio! loro perdonate!

MADDALENA & SPARAFUCILE: Entrate!

MADDALENA: Come in.

GILDA: God! Forgive them!

MADDALENA AND SPARAFUCILE: Come in!

GILDA *enters;* SPARAFUCILE *closes the door behind her, and for some moments the stage is totally dark. During the orchestral passage that follows, the storm worsens, then gradually abates.* RIGOLETTO, *muffled in his cloak, reenters.*

RIGOLETTO: Della vendetta alfin giunge l'istante! Da trenta dì l'aspetto di vivo sangue a lagrime piangendo, sotto la larva del buffon. *(He inspects the house.)* Quest'uscio—è chiuso! Ah, non è tempo ancor. S'attenda. Qual notte di mistero! Una tempesta in cielo! in terra un omicidio! Oh come in vero qui grande mi sento! *(A clock strikes midnight.)* Mezzanotte! *(He knocks.)*

RIGOLETTO: Finally the moment of revenge has arrived! I've waited thirty days for it, weeping tears of hot blood under the jester's mask. *(He inspects the house.)* This door—it's closed! Ah, it's not time yet. Let me wait. What an eerie night! A storm in heaven! a murder on earth! Oh, how I feel like a truly great man! *(A clock strikes midnight.)* Midnight! *(He knocks.)*

SPARAFUCILE: Chi è là?

SPARAFUCILE: Who's there?

RIGOLETTO *(about to enter)*: Son io.

RIGOLETTO *(about to enter)*: It's I.

SPARAFUCILE: Sostate. *(He goes inside and returns, dragging a sack.)* È qua spento il vostr'uomo!

SPARAFUCILE: Wait a minute. *(He goes inside and returns, dragging a sack.)* Here's your man, dead!

RIGOLETTO: Oh gioia! Un lume.

RIGOLETTO: Oh, joy! A light.

SPARAFUCILE: Un lume? No, il danaro. *(*RIGOLETTO *gives him a purse.)* Lesti, all'onda il gettiam.

SPARAFUCILE: A light? No, the money. *(*RIGOLETTO *gives him a purse.)* Quick, let's throw him in the water.

RIGOLETTO: No, basto io solo.

RIGOLETTO: No, I can manage alone.

SPARAFUCILE: Come vi piace. Qui men atto è il sito ... più avanti è più profondo il gorgo. Presto, che alcun non vi sorprenda. Buona notte. *(He reenters the house.)*

SPARAFUCILE: As you please. It isn't as suitable a place here ... further along it's deeper. Hurry, so nobody takes you by surprise. Good night. *(He reenters the house.)*

RIGOLETTO: Egli è là! morto! oh sì! vorrei vederlo! Ma che importa! è ben desso! Ecco i suoi sproni. Ora mi guarda, o mondo! Quest'è un buffone, ed un potente è questo! Ei sta sotto i miei piedi! È desso! oh gioia! È giunta alfine la tua vendetta, o duolo! Sia l'onda a lui sepolcro, un sacco il suo lenzuolo! All'onda! all'onda!

RIGOLETTO: There he is! Dead! oh, yes! I want to see him! But what does it matter! It's himself, all right! There are his spurs. Now look at me, world! This is a jester, and this is a ruler! He is under my feet! It is he! oh, joy! At last your revenge has arrived, o sorrow! Let the river be his grave, a sack his shroud! To the river! to the river!

Just as RIGOLETTO *is about to drag the sack to the water's edge, he hears the voice of the* DUKE, *who crosses at the rear of the stage.*

DUKE: La donna è mobile qual piuma al vento, muta d'accento e di pensiero.

RIGOLETTO: Qual voce!

DUKE: Sempre un amabile, leggiadro viso,—

DUKE: —in pianto o in riso, è menzognero.

RIGOLETTO: Illusion notturna è questa!

DUKE: La donna è mobil qual piuma al vento—

RIGOLETTO *(startled)*: No, no—

DUKE: —muta d'accento e di pensier.

RIGOLETTO: —no! Egli è desso!

RIGOLETTO: Maledizione! *(Turning toward the house:)* Olà —dimon bandito!

DUKE: Woman is fickle as a feather in the breeze, changeable in word and in thought.

RIGOLETTO: That voice!

DUKE: Always a lovable, comely face,—

DUKE: —weeping or smiling, it's deceitful.

RIGOLETTO: This is a deception of the night!

DUKE: Woman is fickle as a feather in the breeze—

RIGOLETTO *(startled)*: No, no—

DUKE: —changeable in word and in thought.

RIGOLETTO: —no! It's himself!

RIGOLETTO: Damn you! *(Turning toward the house:)* Over there —robber fiend!

DUKE *(fading into the distance)*: Muta d'accento e di pensier, e di pensier, e di pensier.

RIGOLETTO: Chi è mai, chi è qui in sua vece? *(He opens the sack.)* Io tremo, È umano corpo. Mia figlia! Dio! mia figlia! *(Lightning flashes.)* Ah no! È impossibil! Per Verona è in via! Fu vision! È dessa! *(He kneels.)* Oh mia Gilda! Fanciulla! a me rispondi! L'assassino mi svela ... *(He rushes toward the inn door and beats on it frantically.)* Olà? Nessuno? nessun! Mia figlia? mia Gilda? oh, mia figlia?

GILDA: Chi mi chiama?

RIGOLETTO: Ella parla! si move! È viva! oh Dio! Ah, mio ben solo in terra ... Mi guarda—mi conosci—

GILDA: Ah padre mio!

RIGOLETTO: Qual mistero! che fu! Sei tu ferita? Dimmi—

GILDA: L'acciar—qui *(Pointing to her heart:)*—qui mi piagò.

RIGOLETTO: Chi t'ha colpita?

GILDA: V'ho ingannato ... colpevole fui ... l'amai troppo ... ora muoio per lui!

DUKE *(fading into the distance)*: Changeable in word and in thought, and in thought, and in thought.

RIGOLETTO: Whoever is it that is here in his place? *(He opens the sack.)* I'm trembling. It's a human body. My daughter! God! my daughter! *(Lightning flashes.)* Ah no! It's impossible! She's on her way to Verona! It was an apparition! It's she herself! *(He kneels.)* Oh, my Gilda! my child! answer me! Tell me your murderer ... *(He rushes toward the inn door and beats on it frantically.)* Hey there? Nobody? nobody! My daughter? my Gilda? oh, my daughter?

GILDA: Who calls me?

RIGOLETTO: She speaks! She moves! She's alive! Oh God! Ah, my only joy in the world ... Look at me—recognize me—

GILDA: Ah, my father!

RIGOLETTO: What a mystery! What happened? Are you hurt? Tell me—

GILDA: The sword wounded me here *(Pointing to her heart:)*—here.

RIGOLETTO: Who stabbed you?

GILDA: I deceived you ... it was my fault ... I loved him too much ... now I'm dying for him!

RIGOLETTO *(to himself)*: (Dio tremendo! ella stessa fu colta dallo stral di mia giusta vendetta!) *(To* GILDA:*)* Angiol caro—mi guarda, m'ascolta—Parla, parlami, figlia diletta!

RIGOLETTO *(to himself)*: (Great God! She herself was struck by the arrow of my rightful revenge!) *(To* GILDA:*)* Dear angel—look at me, listen to me— Speak, speak to me, darling daughter!

GILDA: Ah, ch'io taccia! A me—a lui perdonate! Benedite alla figlia, o mio padre! Lassù in cielo, vicina alla madre—in eterno per voi pregherò.

GILDA: Ah, that I might be silent! Forgive me—him! Bless your daughter, o my father! Up there in heaven, beside my mother—I'll pray for you everlastingly.

RIGOLETTO: Non morir, mio tesoro—pietade ... Mia colomba, lasciarmi non dêi, no, lasciarmi non dêi!

RIGOLETTO: Don't die, my treasure—for pity's sake ... My dove, you mustn't leave me, no, you mustn't leave me!

GILDA: Lassù in cielo, vicina alla madre—

GILDA: Up there in heaven, beside my mother—

RIGOLETTO: Oh mia figlia!

RIGOLETTO: Oh, my daughter!

GILDA: —in eterno per voi pregherò—

GILDA: —I'll pray for you eternally—

RIGOLETTO: No, lasciarmi non dêi—

RIGOLETTO: No, you mustn't leave me—

GILDA: —pregherò—

GILDA: —I'll pray—

RIGOLETTO: —non morir—

RIGOLETTO: —don't die—

GILDA: —per voi pregherò.

GILDA: —I'll pray for you.

RIGOLETTO: —se t'involi, qui sol, qui sol rimarrei— Non morire, o qui teco morrò!

RIGOLETTO: —if you cease to be, I'll remain here alone, here alone— Don't die, or I'll die here with you!

GILDA: Non più ... A lui ...

GILDA: No more ... To him ...

RIGOLETTO: Oh, mia figlia!

RIGOLETTO: Oh, my daughter!

GILDA: Perdonate—

GILDA: Forgiveness—

RIGOLETTO: Oh, mia Gilda!

RIGOLETTO: Oh, my Gilda!

GILDA: —mio padre—

RIGOLETTO: No, lasciarmi non dêi!

GILDA: —addio!

GILDA: Lassù in ciel—

RIGOLETTO: Non morir—

GILDA: —lassù in ciel—

RIGOLETTO: No, lasciarmi non dêi—

GILDA: —pregherò—

RIGOLETTO: —non morir!

GILDA: —per voi preghe— *(She dies.)*

RIGOLETTO: Gilda! mia Gilda! È morta! Ah! La maledizione!

GILDA: —my father—

RIGOLETTO: No, you mustn't leave me!

GILDA: —goodbye!

GILDA: Up there in heaven—

RIGOLETTO: Don't die—

GILDA: —up there in heaven—

RIGOLETTO: No, you mustn't leave me—

GILDA: —I'll pray—

RIGOLETTO: —don't die!

GILDA: —I'll pray for y—*(She dies.)*

RIGOLETTO: Gilda! my Gilda! She's dead! Ah! The curse!

Tearing his hair, he falls on his daughter's body.